TEXT AND PERFORMANCE

General Editor: Michael Scott

The series is designed to introduce sixth-form and under-graduate students to the themes, continuing vitality and performance of major dramatic works. The attention given to production aspects is an element of special importance, responding to the invigoration given to literary study by the work of leading contemporary critics.

The prime aim is to present each play as a vital experience in the mind of the reader – achieved by analysis of the text in relation to its themes and theatricality. Emphasis is accordingly placed on the relevance of the work to the modern reader and the world of today. At the same time, traditional views are presented and appraised, forming the basis from which a creative response to the text can develop.

In each volume, Part One: *Text* discusses key themes or problems, the reader being encouraged to gain a stronger perception both of the inherent character of the work and also of variations in interpreting it. Part Two: *Performance* examines the ways in which these themes or problems have been handled in modern productions, and the approaches and techniques employed to enhance the play's accessibility to modern audiences.

A synopsis of the play is given and an outline of its major sources, and a concluding Reading List offers guidance to the student's independent study of the work.

DOCTOR FAUSTUS

Text and Performance

WILLIAM TYDEMAN

002117 **M**

MACMILLAN

First published 1984

Published by
Higher and Further Education Division
MACMILLAN PUBLISHERS LTD
Houndmills, Basingstoke, Hampshire RG21 2XS
and London
Companies and representatives
throughout the world

Typeset by
Wessex Typesetters Ltd
Frome, Somerset

Printed in Hong Kong

British Library Cataloguing in Publication Data
Tydeman, William,
Doctor Faustus.–(Text and performance)
1. Marlowe, Christopher, *1564–1593*.
Doctor Faustus
I. Title   II. Series
822′.3   PR2664
ISBN 0–333–34313–1

CONTENTS

Illustrations will be found in Part Two

ACKNOWLEDGEMENTS

My sincere thanks are due to the General Editor for his enthusiasm and encouragement; to the staff of the British Theatre Museum and Marion O'Connor for expert assistance; to Vesna Pistotnik of the Shakespeare Institute, University of Birmingham, for generously sharing with me results from her detailed researches. Joyce Williams and Ann McCallum have deciphered and typed a much-revised manuscript. Critical works referred to in the text are gratefully cited in the Select Reading List; I owe a great deal to many that are not. References to *Doctor Faustus* are taken from J. D. Jump's invaluable Revels Plays edition of 1962.

Source details for the illustrations are given with the relevant captions to the photographs. Every effort has been made to trace all the copyright-holders but if any have been inadvertently overlooked, the publishers will be pleased to make the necessary arrangements.

GENERAL EDITOR'S PREFACE

For many years a mutual suspicion existed between the theatre director and the literary critic of drama. Although in the first half of the century there were important exceptions, such was the rule. A radical change of attitude, however, has taken place over the last thirty years. Critics and directors now increasingly recognise the significance of each other's work and acknowledge their growing awareness of interdependence. Both interpret the same text, but do so according to their different situations and functions. Without the director, the designer and the actor, a play's existence is only partial. They revitalise the text with action, enabling the drama to live fully at each performance. The academic critic investigates the script to elucidate its textual problems, understand its conventions and discover how it operates. He may also propose his view of the work, expounding what he considers to be its significance.

Dramatic texts belong therefore to theatre and to literature. The aim of the 'Text and Performance' series is to achieve a fuller recognition of how both enhance our enjoyment of the play. Each volume follows the same basic pattern. Part One provides a critical introduction to the play under discussion, using the techniques and criteria of the literary critic in examining the manner in which the work operates through language, imagery and action. Part Two takes the enquiry further into the play's theatricality by focusing on selected productions of recent times so as to illustrate points of contrast and comparison in the interpretation of different directors and actors, and to demonstrate how the drama has worked on the modern stage. In this way the series seeks to provide a lively and informative introduction to major plays in their text and performance.

MICHAEL SCOTT

PLOT SYNOPSIS AND SOURCE

Doctor Faustus exists in two main versions, the A-text (1604) and the B-text (1616). The chief differences are discussed briefly in the 'Text' section below. This synopsis follows the scene-divisions of Jump's Revels Plays edition (1962), which is based on the B-text. Where the A-version differs significantly, Jump prints it in an Appendix; in the synopsis the main divergences are noted in square brackets. To facilitate reference to other editions, the numeration of J. B. Steane's Penguin text is also given. Asterisks [*] indicate scenes agreed to be mainly or wholly attributable to Marlowe.

Prologue.* The Chorus describes F's youth, academic success, and recourse to magic.

Scene i (I 1)* F reviews his career, and resolving to take up necromancy, summons Valdes and Cornelius to further his researches.

Scene ii (I 2)* Two of F's fellow-scholars learn of his doings from his servant Wagner.

Scene iii (I 3)* F successfully conjures up Mephostophilis, and informs him that he wishes to strike a bargain with Lucifer.

Scene iv (I 4)* Wagner persuades the Clown Robin to serve him, offering to teach him to conjure. [In A the scene is lengthened by additional badinage.]

Scene v (I 5)* F, advised by his Good and Bad Angels, signs a bond with Lucifer, despite warning phenomena. Hell is discussed, and F punished for demanding a wife. He is given magic books.

[A scene may be lost here, showing Robin deserting Wagner to work at an inn as an ostler.]

Scene vi (II 1)* F is assailed by qualms of conscience, but an astronomical discussion with Mephostophilis, and a pageant of the Seven Deadly Sins, divert him.

Scene vii (II 2)* Robin and Dick, another servant, plan to raise spirits with the help of one of F's books. [In A this scene, inserted prior to Scene x, runs into it; the servant is Rafe or Ralph; more sexual innuendo occurs.]

Chorus 1 (III 1)* The Chorus [in A Wagner] speaks of F's astronomical observations, his travels through space, his geographical survey, his visit to Rome.

Scene viii (III 2) Mephostophilis and F describe their tour; they visit the Pope who [not in A] has just subdued his rival Bruno. F and Mephostophilis disguised as cardinals take a hand in the proceedings. [A makes a single shorter scene of parts of Scenes viii and ix.]

Scene ix (III 3) The now invisible F and Mephostophilis disrupt the papal banquet. The Friars formally curse F.

Scene x (III 4) Robin and Dick steal a goblet from a Vintner; they summon Mephostophilis to protect them, but he punishes them. [In A the business is briefer.]

Chorus 2.   F's exploits have won him fame, and he comes to the notice of the Emperor Charles V, at whose court we next view him. [This speech is not in B; A prints it after Scene ix.]

Scene xi (IV 1)   [Not in A.] Two imperial courtiers are anxious to inspect F, but their friend Benvolio has a hangover and is surly.

Scene xii (IV 2)   Conjuring up Alexander the Great and his mistress to please the Emperor, F humiliates Benvolio for his derision; the latter vows revenge. [In A the action is more compact; Benvolio becomes an anonymous 'Knight'.]

Scene xiii (IV 3)   [Not in A.] Benvolio and his friends plan to avenge the insult, but are discomforted by the doctor and Mephostophilis, who escape injury.

Scene xiv (IV 4)   [Not in A.] The courtiers reappear, partially transformed to animals. They retire in shame from public view.

Scene xv (IV 5)   F sells a Horse-Courser a magic steed which turns into a bundle of hay; the dealer seizes F's leg which comes off and the man runs away in fright. [In A the scene is lengthened, notably in the Horse-Courser's role.]

Scene xvi (IV 6)   [Not in A.] At a tavern a Carter and the Horse-Courser tell Dick, Robin, and the Hostess how F has tricked them.

Scene xvii (IV 7)   F displays his powers before the Duke and Duchess of Vanholt, but [in B only] is interrupted by his victims demanding retribution. F strikes them all dumb.

Scene xviii (V 1)*   F makes a will, feasts his friends, and conjures up Helen of Troy. A virtuous Old Man pleads with him to repent, but Mephostophilis frightens F into reaffirming his fidelity to Lucifer. F asks for Helen as his mistress, and she returns. The Old Man laments F's recalcitrance.

Scene xix (V 2)*   Lucifer and his crew gloat [not in A] as F bids his friends farewell, and his final hour on earth runs its course. As midnight strikes, the devils carry him off to Hell.

Scene xx (V 3)*   [Not in A.] F's fellow-scholars visit his room, discovering his dismembered corpse. They lament his death, and plan his funeral.

Epilogue.*   The Chorus sums up F's life, and moralises on his fate.

SOURCE

The Historie of the damnable life, and deserved death of Doctor John Faustus (1592), English translation by 'P. F. Gent.' of the *Historia von D. Johann Fausten* (Frankfurt, 1587), which consolidated various forms of the legend current in late medieval Germany.

TO THE MEMORY
OF
FRANK W. BRADBROOK
(1917–83)
COLLEAGUE AND FRIEND

PART ONE: TEXT

1 INTRODUCTION

Only in the last few decades has *Doctor Faustus* regained on the English stage a popularity it evidently enjoyed in the years between its composition around 1592 and the closing of London's playhouses fifty years later. Because, happily, this earliest of great Elizabethan tragedies is now often performed, contemporary playgoers are in a better position to assess its qualities for themselves than were those who could only judge Marlowe's work from 'the words on the page'. While scholars and critics have always kept debate about the play's content fruitfully alive, today, as a result of the achievements of directors and actors, Marlowe's most complex drama has emerged from theatrical obscurity to excite and engage live audiences too.

Doctor Faustus is obviously of major literary and dramatic importance, however little agreement there may be as to its precise excellences. This is not unusual with monuments of dramatic art, as all readers of *Hamlet* are acutely aware: essential greatness is not impaired by a multiplicity of opinions as to what that greatness consists of. As with *Hamlet*, the definitive 'meaning' of *Faustus* can never be pinned down once and for all. Great art grows with us, and our belief as to 'what it signifies' may shift several times not simply within one lifespan, but even during a single reading or performance. Adopt a rigidly orthodox viewpoint, and Faustus's presumption in attempting to flout his creator's edicts deserves everlasting damnation in Hell. Approach the work in a militantly humanistic spirit, and the scholar's venture into the unknown becomes a desperate but justifiable means of expanding his physical and intellectual horizons. Faustus's thwarted aspirations have been identified with those of the typical 'New Man' of the European Renaissance, confident in his bodily and mental attributes, demanding the right to know with Mac-

beth's insistent claim that he 'will be satisfied', only to be
cruelly frustrated. But should we rather read *Faustus* as a
prophetic parable anticipating the selfish amorality of scientific
materialism, prepared to sacrifice life itself in the ruthless
pursuit of power through knowledge? Or is it an allegory of our
mortal condition, the dissection of a species doomed to dream
of reaching summits of achievement its fallible constitution
must always deny it?

Our impression of the play as a dramatic experience must
involve an assessment of its leading figure as a dramatic
character. Faustus himself is an amalgam of seemingly contradictory traits, a complex creation to which we respond
almost as we do to a living acquaintance whose life-style and
attitudes fascinate yet baffle us. To some Faustus is a self-
centred hedonist whose sole aim is personal gratification,
mental or sensual; to others he is a spiritual pioneer, seeking to
clear away the obstacles placed in the way of mankind's
progress by a repressive god. Is Faustus an adolescent dreamer
indulging in reveries of immortality and omniscience, or does
he represent that laudable impulse by which we strive to
overcome our human limitations through acts of necessary if
reckless courage? Is he frantic libertine, fearless liberator, or
both? Marlowe's capacity for building a figure whose conduct
and opinions can produce in us changing emotions and
conflicting judgements typifies the increasing subtlety of
sixteenth-century English dramatic literature as it attains its
zenith in the work of William Shakespeare.

This developing sophistication is perhaps less obviously seen
in the way Marlowe planned and shaped the course of the
action. Although his source supplied him with the main
features of Faustus's career, to construct the play still required
of him a flair for selecting appropriate incidents and an instinct
for making them theatrically effective. The confident fluency of
the opening scenes and the one in which Faustus is finally
destroyed conceals much technical skill and linguistic resource-
fulness. More taxing to accomplish successfully was the task of
linking the structural pinnacle of Faustus's pact with Lucifer
with that of the hour of retribution, and not all agree that
Marlowe was equal to the challenge. Many account for the
presumed discrepancy in expression and technique between

the proud grandeur of the protagonist's initial ambitions or the awful anguish of his last hours, and what appears as the inane sensationalism and pointless foolery of the intervening scenes, by arguing that whoever invented the latter failed to appreciate the loftiness of Marlowe's overall design. But Elizabethan drama was a hybrid organism, and, even if Marlowe did not actually write all the offending scenes himself, they were doubtless planned and perhaps partly executed by him. It has even been argued that the middle portion of the play is less 'mean and grovelling' than William Hazlitt once suggested, and that to an Elizabethan audience Faustus's daring exploits and magical skills would have seemed impressive and far from mere cheap trickery. At least these actions keep Marlowe's hero on the brink of repentance and distract spectators from his peril until damnation is ensured. Others go further and regard the 'inferior' scenes not simply as theatrically necessary, but as central to a critical appreciation of the entire work. For them the obvious banality and futility of what Faustus accomplishes following the pact-signing form a deliberately ironic variation on the perennial theme of the Vanity of Human Wishes. A man with a fine record of worldly success, Faustus upon the acquisition of virtually infinite power and infinite knowledge can find little better to do with his dearly bought skills than throw fireworks at friars and supply pregnant duchesses with fruit out of season.

Close attention must also be paid to the vital role performed by language in the play. Glib reference to 'Marlowe's mighty line' can become something of an evasive cliché, and recent scrutiny has been devoted less to the sonorous splendours of the set-speeches than to the subtler aspects of Marlowe's linguistic practice. Colourful and exquisitely delicate poetry does feature in *Doctor Faustus* – the hero's invocation to Helen of Troy opens with the most revered line in the whole Marlovian canon – but such beauties must be related to their context rather than admired in isolation from it. Moreover, alongside passages of lyrical melody more satisfying to the ear than almost anything English audiences had heard before, and resonant oratory with 'everie word' (as Robert Greene sneered) 'filling the mouth like the Faburden of Bo-bell', Marlowe evolved a speech idiom for his manic-depressive hero charged with a unique individuality.

Tense, brash, nervous, dynamic, uneasily jocular by turns, this
mode of diction is as far removed from Greene's caricature of
Marlowe's style, as are those exchanges of quietly ironic
dialogue which belie the myth that Marlowe only scored his
plays for drums-and-trumpets.

Not everyone has admired the tragedy of *Faustus*. There are
still those to whom, as to the Victorians, Marlowe is more poet
than playwright, and for whom his theatrical talent remains
crude, elementary, or non-existent. These matters can only be
truly tested on a stage before an audience, and not every recent
revival of Marlowe's plays has confirmed that his was an
unvaryingly dramatic gift. Some commentators continue to
assert that his plays are unbalanced achievements, that they
leave too many situations obscure and too many characters
insufficiently motivated to be understood, that they reveal too
little care in composition to be accorded the highest honours.
These charges, where they apply to *Doctor Faustus*, will also be
confronted and discussed in the pages that follow.

The A- and B-Texts

Doctor Faustus has one of the most exceptionally complicated
textual histories in Elizabethan literature. The primary problem in discussing any aspect of this play is that it survives in two
related but differing versions, neither of which accurately
represents the text as Marlowe and a probable collaborator
first wrote it. This initial difficulty has to be tackled before we
can start to consider questions of interpretation, or features of
structure or style. And, of course, matters of textual preference
assume an important role when we come to analyse performances too.

The earliest surviving text of *Doctor Faustus* appeared in 1604,
some twelve years after its most likely date of composition. This
version, reprinted in 1609 and 1611 and known to scholars as
the A-text, is possibly not the first edition of the work ever
printed, given the attested popularity of the piece, the knowledge that publication was sanctioned as early as 7 January
1601, and the fact that the title-page bears the former name of
an acting-company which played under a new patron from

1603. In 1616 another fuller version of *Faustus*, since christened the B-text, was published, and these two editions constitute the sole access we possess to Marlowe and friend's original script of 1592–3. Unfortunately, it is now clear that the A-text omits or corrupts much of what was originally presented on stage, while the B-text, although more faithful to the early script, includes a good deal of material added after Marlowe's death in 1593.

To understand how this could come about we have to remember that in the Elizabethan period few dramatic authors bothered to preserve duplicate copies of their work for their personal files, possible publication, or posterity. The writer's draft manuscript ('foul papers') or a fair copy, once sold to an acting-company for performance, became company property and usually passed out of the playwright's ken. Though some writers held on to their 'foul papers', the custom of outright purchase meant that an author had little control over the ultimate fate of his creation, let alone the manuscript the players had bought off him. Transcribed to form the prompt-book or acting-script, the work could be added to, subtracted from, revised, or rearranged, all without the writer's approval or knowledge. This being so, it is easy to comprehend why the original *Doctor Faustus* is inadequately represented by both the 1604 and 1616 versions that survive.

The textual details are tortuous to grasp, but a simplified version might run like this: the piece probably belonged first to the Earl of Pembroke's Men, one of the numerous professional acting-companies of Elizabethan London. They may have acted it at court during the winter of 1592–3, and at the Theatre in Shoreditch during January 1593 before the severe plague of that year shut the playhouses. Later that year Pembroke's prompt-book of *Faustus* was purchased, probably by Philip Henslowe, impressario and manager of the Lord Admiral's Men, whose patron, Lord Howard of Effingham, had led Elizabeth's fleet against the Armada. The first recorded performance of the play, at the Rose Theatre, Bankside, on 30 September 1594, was given by the Lord Admiral's Men, with Edward Alleyn in the leading role. Numerous presentations followed well into the seventeenth century.

The A-text of 1604 represents an abbreviated version of *Doctor Faustus* as first acted, imperfectly put together from memory by actors (Pembroke's Men?) and cut down for touring performances in the provinces. Inevitably, the A-text preserved some portions of the original play better than others, the tragic parts being more accurately recollected than the comic ones. Even so, the 1616 text is much fuller than that of 1604, containing some 604 additional lines of print which flesh out episodes that the earlier edition merely sketches in. These include Faustus's exploits at the papal and imperial courts, the incidents involving the Horse-Courser at the tavern and in the Duke of Vanholt's residence, and the final scenes which in the B-text call for a number of technical devices unlikely to have been available on a provincial tour. The fact that A supplies some of the 'low-life' episodes in more detail than B suggests unauthorised expansions of the 1592–3 script through the company's comedians speaking more than was set down for them.

Most scholars, led by Sir Walter Greg, see the 1616 edition as coming closer to Marlowe's original than the 1604 version, believing that its compiler had access to Marlowe's 'foul papers', supplementing them with the 1611 edition of the A-text where the manuscript was damaged or defective. Today, however, many experts feel that Greg was in error in thinking that the B-text supplied no more than the gist of the original as it left Marlowe's hands. It now seems clear that B not only includes much of the 1592–3 text, but also incorporates the numerous 'adicyones' for which Henslowe paid two minor dramatists, Rowley and Birde, £4 on 22 November 1602.

Thus neither extant text of *Doctor Faustus* is entirely uncorrupted. Yet the existence of two differing versions does serve to remind us of the tremendous popularity of the play, whichever text the public was invited to respond to in performance.

2 'What Doctrine Call You This?'

Critical opinion has rarely been united as to the appropriate response to *Doctor Faustus*. In the same year (1817) that Henry Maitland, arguing that Faustus harmed no one but himself, could pronounce his fate undeserved, Francis Jeffrey endorsed the fall of 'a vulgar sorcerer, tempted to sell his soul to the Devil for the ordinary price of sensual pleasure, and earthly power and glory'. As the nineteenth century wore on, however, general opinion strengthened that the quality of the scholar's passionate desires and of the language in which they found expression easily counteracted his impious temerity in sealing a bond with the Devil. For Francis Cunningham in 1870 the last hour of the doctor's life filled the soul 'with love and admiration for a departed hero'; for J. A. Symonds, Faustus, 'the medieval rebel', was animated by Marlowe's 'own audacious spirit', and in 1887 Havelock Ellis exalted Faustus as 'a living man thirsting for the infinite'. Such eulogies continued into the present century, Una Ellis-Fermor discovering in him 'dignity, patience, tenacity and a certain profundity of thought' while by 1932 F. S. Boas was applying to a Faustus cast in his creator's image Horatio's tribute to the dead Hamlet: 'Now cracks a noble heart'.

The most extreme statement of this view emanated in 1910 from the American philosopher George Santayana, for whom 'this excellent Faustus' was a good Protestant, 'damned by accident or predestination'. He goes on,

> we see an essentially good man, because in a moment of infatuation he had signed away his soul, driven against his will to despair and damnation. . . . The evil angel represents the natural ideal of Faustus, or of any child of the Renaissance; he appeals to the vague but healthy ambitions of a young soul, that would make trial of the world. In other words, the devil represents the true good, and it is no wonder if the honest Faustus cannot resist his suggestions. We like him for his love of life, for his trust in nature, for his enthusiasm for beauty. . . . Marlowe's Faustus is a martyr to everything that the Renaissance prized, – power, curious knowledge, enterprise, wealth, and beauty.
>
> (*Three Philosophical Poets*, 1910, pp. 147–9)

Some may consider such an approach partisan and partial, but the spirit behind these claims bears witness to a general belief in Faustus's fundamental significance as a human being. He is not a cipher to whose aspirations or plight we can remain indifferent. While not necessarily endorsing Santayana's fervent testimony, most of us find more to Faustus than simply an

arrogant, foolish, immature or blasphemous man whose appetites betray him into overreaching himself, as both Prologue
and Epilogue would have us believe.

However, if we are unable to simplify his fate as the
inevitable come-uppance of a self-centred hedonist who flouts
God's just laws, it is another thing to portray Faustus as more
sinned against than sinning, as one whose intellectual ardour
and aesthetic awareness justify his 'disobedience'. Such a view
has persisted, however, and Nicholas Brooke's essay 'The
Moral Tragedy of Doctor Faustus' remains its most sophisti-
cated and discerning exposition. Brooke regards Faustus as one
who sets out to achieve 'the supreme desires of Man',
describing these as 'the only positive ideas advanced' in the
play and seeing the magnificence with which they are endowed
as obliterating all the trite moral exhortations. Admitting that
Faustus's ambitions are formulated as a jumble of disparate
pursuits, Brooke still insists that 'all the positive statements of
the play, supported by the finest verse, are against the declared
Christian moral', while statements which advance the
'heavenly' case remain 'vague, flat, meaningless'. For this critic
the piece becomes an inverted morality play in which Faustus
appears justified in refusing to assume a position of humble
servitude to God. Even the traditional technique of introducing
Good and Bad Angels becomes a device for satirising the divine
régime through anachronism. The hero's rejection of Heaven
for Helen of Troy is construed as an act of glorious defiance,
placing appetite above intellect, and exposing the full irony of a
creation which can only fulfil its highest potential by bypassing
God's laws and paying the price. Brooke insists that Faustus's
bargain does bring worthwhile satisfactions with it, and that
his actions in the central scenes appear trivial only because it
was impossible to demonstrate him exercising a command of
the secrets of astronomy and cosmography in adequately
theatrical ways.

Brooke's reading of the play deserves careful thought, but we
may still feel that it ignores the less laudable traits in Faustus's
behaviour, and the less noble aspects of his ambition. Over
against Brooke we have to set the ardent belief of other critics
that *Faustus* remains predominantly an updated medieval
morality play which may accord its protagonist an individual

name and personality, but which still presents his story as that of an archetypal sinful man recompensed for his wicked acts in the traditional manner. Those who hold this opinion point to the overtly Christian imagery and machinery of the play, the terminology of Faustus's final soliloquy, the stern language of the Prologue and Epilogue: 'swollen with cunning of a self-conceit' [Prologue, 20]; 'falling to a devilish exercise' [ibid., 23]; 'Cut is the branch that might have grown full straight' [Epilogue, 1].

Thus amid Victorian adulation in 1877 Wilhelm Wagner wrote, 'Marlowe's Faustus is anything but a hero . . . though we can sympathise with his fear and lamentations, yet we cannot but feel that his end is the appropriate conclusion of his career.' In more recent years others have adopted the view that it is only by dint of an excess of critical sophistication that *Faustus* can be interpreted as anything other than an admonitory drama, however skilfully varied from its medieval predecessors. James Smith in 'Marlowe's *Doctor Faustus*' and Greg in 'The Damnation of Faustus' argue in favour of such an interpretation, which Leo Kirschbaum in 'Marlowe's *Faustus*: A Reconsideration' expresses trenchantly if a little too forcefully. Castigating the doctor as a 'blatant egotist . . . self-deluded, foolishly boastful', and 'a wretched creature who for lower values gives up higher values', Kirschbaum concludes, 'The Christian view of the world informs *Dr Faustus* throughout – not the pagan view. . . . Whatever Marlowe was himself, there is no more obvious Christian document in all Elizabethan drama than *Dr Faustus*.'

Typical is the attention which such critics pay to Faustus's encounter with Helen of Troy in Scene xviii. Arguing that his off-stage copulation with a disguised demon (which they take Helen to be) is the ultimate act that puts salvation irrevocably beyond his reach, they attach great importance at line 102 to his cry of 'Her lips suck forth my soul', and to the blasphemy of the preceding request that she should make him immortal with a kiss. Sexual intercourse with a demon has been taken to be a damnable offence, and Kirschbaum, Greg and others highlight the Old Man's comment in lines 119–21 as Faustus leads Helen off:

Accursed Faustus, miserable man,
That from thy soul exclud'st the grace of heaven
And fliest the throne of his tribunal seat!

Yet several commentators have challenged this reading, arguing, like J. C. Maxwell in 'The Sin of Faustus', that it
overemphasises Faustus's sin of sensuality rather than pride,
or, like T. W. Craik in 'Faustus' Damnation Reconsidered',
that the Old Man's valediction does not necessarily refer to
copulation with a demon, which does not necessarily follow
Faustus's exit with Helen. Moreover, Nicholas Kiessling in
'Doctor Faustus and the Sin of Demoniality' points out that the
Second Scholar still holds out the hope of salvation after Helen
has become Faustus's mistress, and that sex with a demonic
spirit was never considered as being 'beyond redemption'.

So, while there is much to support a reading of *Faustus* on
strict morality lines, there is evidence to refute it too. For one
thing Faustus is a complicated human being whose motives for
behaving as he does, while not explicit, are none the less
discernible and plausible. Unlike the earlier morality hero, he
is no one-dimensional creation without a psychology: we
recognise our common humanity in him, and, even though we
may disapprove of what he does, most of us acknowledge that
his fate cannot be explained entirely satisfactorily as that of a
wicked sinner whose end induces in us a smug feeling that we
have seen justice done. Faustus is sympathetic and credible
enough for us to believe that his downfall results from a human
failure, like that of Macbeth or Oedipus, to understand the
enormity of what he is proposing to himself; he is an unhappy
figure who acts against his own better nature, and whose
agonised death is a matter for regret rather than applause. This
is what gives him tragic stature for all his personal weaknesses
and defects.

What is the theme of the play which bears Faustus's name?
Some might reply that it is to be found in humanity's blindness
to the reality of its own immortal essence, that in thinking Hell
a fable and his own soul a trifle Faustus is denying the spiritual
truth about himself. Others, unable to adopt a position
essentially Christian and yet unwilling to surrender entirely to
the allure of Brooke's portrait of the martyred humanist, find

the core of the tragedy in the Epilogue's first line. For them 'Cut is the branch that might have grown full straight' epitomises that sense of human wastage and avoidable pain lying at the root of all tragic art. The man who might have lived contentedly and profitably lies dead, having dared the impossible and lost. To such people the fact that Faustus enlisted diabolic aid is probably less important today than his pathetic need to transcend his own limitations. Perhaps at the base of Faustus's tragedy lies a fundamental inability to accept himself as a man, a self-disgust at discovering himself to be human after all. If he ends 'cut off from all contact with humanity', as Brooke suggests, it could be his own fault for seeking to become more than human in the first instance.

Failed Superman or foolish sinner? Each of us can privately resolve the debate, but the choice is ours, for Marlowe does not attempt to influence us one way or the other. Preserving a neutral stance, he leaves us free to make up our own minds. In this he shows himself a pioneer by comparison with his immediate predecessors in the field of English drama, and appreciation of this remarkable fact can also assist us to accept Marlowe's ambivalent presentation of his hero's dilemma.

Most early sixteenth-century drama was didactic: it sought less to examine problems of human behaviour and personal conduct than to illustrate the consequences of right- and wrong-doing. Only slowly did dramatists show interest in ethical complications or moral predicaments, in what led people to behave antisocially or in ways which the Church deemed worthy of punishment here or in the afterlife. Plays generally upheld the belief that men and women were free agents confronted by a choice between two modes of living, one acceptable and encouraged, the other unacceptable and condemned. No extenuating circumstances could be permitted to mitigate wrongdoing, no explanatory pleas could disguise the commission of sins. Last-minute repentance might secure last-minute salvation, but it was not the business of drama to question the hallowed system of rewards and punishments, to challenge the traditional pieties, or to explore the moral, spiritual, or psychological reasons which had led an individual to select the wrong path.

Marlowe lived in an age and moved in circles which had

started to query the old orthodoxies, and he, like many thinking people of his day, could not fail to be aware of the new agencies at work in the Western world, guaranteeing mankind more say in its own future, boosting its confidence in its own abilities and in its right to shape its own environment. The rigidly limited and defined 'world-picture' beloved of medieval thinkers was being dismembered, and Renaissance men and women were left contemplating in bewilderment the clash between the outdated but still reassuring cosmic framework familiarised by tradition, and a more scientifically demonstrable pattern which was still alarmingly novel and untried. Little wonder that John Donne could comment in *An Anatomie of the World* (1611) that 'wise nature'

> observ'd that every sort of men
> Did in their voyage in this worlds Sea stray
> And needed a new compasse for their way.   [224–6]

Marlowe was acutely aware of the predictably mixed reactions of his contemporaries to the fresh set of dilemmas which 'the pressures of modern life' posed for them. For many the changes in politics, religion and morality, the almost daily discoveries in the natural world and in the realm of ideas, the unleashing of acquisitive and aspiring instincts in social and economic affairs, would have seemed unsettling and unacceptable, forcing them to cling resolutely to old beliefs and opinions. Others, eager to embrace the 'new Philosophy', were convinced that, the sooner the old mental lumber was got rid of and man's energies were released from guilt-ridden restraints, the sooner a brave new world would come into being in which humanity could enjoy a more fulfilled existence.

Without some understanding of the divided mind of the English Renaissance, one cannot fully appreciate *Doctor Faustus*, which typifies the transition from the old black-and-white ethical scheme which underlies the morality play and conditions its audience's judgement, and the more empirical, exploratory investigation of moral issues and psychological conditions which we associate with the best Elizabethan and Jacobean dramas. Marlowe invites us to see the splendour of man, but to contemplate the species at its most abject too. In Kenneth Clark's study *The Nude* (1956) he contrasts the physical perfection of the Hellenic ideal of nudity with that depicted in the naked figures of such Gothic artists as Van Eyck and Dürer, likening these to 'roots and bulbs, pulled up into the light . . . out of the protective darkness'. Both concepts are present in *Faustus*: on one hand we have the boldly defiant, self-reliant figure of the opening, a man of boundless confidence whose egotism is at once awe-inspiring and terrible; on the other hand we find in the Faustus of the close a pitiful, grovelling creature seeking to hide from the consequences of his ambition in the bowels of the earth, vulnerable and stripped of all dignity and self-assurance.

On one level *Doctor Faustus* may be treated as a study of the split personality of the Renaissance; on another as an exploration of just what controls human beings should expect to find placed on their own development given such limiting factors as character and environment. Marlowe has left us ample room for speculation on the issues involved. The Prologue to *Tamburlaine* invites spectators to applaud its hero's fortunes as they please; that to *Faustus* suggests that we assess the scholar's fortunes as 'good or bad'. Preserving authorial neutrality on these matters, Marlowe created a revolution in English drama by refusing to pass overt judgement on his leading figure's conduct. Prologue and Epilogue may speak harshly of Faustus, but the play itself compels us to ponder and debate and decide for ourselves where the key to the truth lies. Its author will not arbitrate for us. All he does is present the paradox of the clash between human aspiration and the restrictions placed on it not only by an inexorable theological scheme but by human fallibility too.

3 'And This the Man'

Marlowe did not invent his hero but inherited him from the demotic mythology of the recent European past. The dark and dubious deeds of Johann Faust caught the popular imagination of Northern Europe during the second half of the sixteenth century, offering an up-to-date version of the long-current tradition of men who, dissatisfied with normal prowess, made contact with the powers of darkness. Tales involving diabolic concessions and human forfeits were grafted onto the actual exploits of two German necromancers who won fame in the 1500s, disappearing around 1540. For adherents of the newly established Lutheran faith, Faust's alleged nefariousness served as an object lesson on the wickedness of abusing God-given talents, and a warning of the disastrous fate to which an insatiable zeal for knowledge might lead, if not tempered with a becoming humility.

Alongside this image of the overambitious apostate stood that of his *alter ego*, an unscrupulous, resourceful Smart Aleck who tricked, jested or brazened his way out of every tight corner he got into. As a result, in the seminal work which brought Faust to international prominence this leading magus also features as charlatan and confidence-trickster. The anonymous *Historia von D. Johann Fausten*, the so-called German *Faustbuch*, published in 1587 at Frankfurt-am-Main, not only bequeathed to its successors the overall account of the rise and fall of an earnest savant, but also a welter of jest-book anecdotes, magical feats and shady deals, which remained part of the Faust *persona* right up to the present century.

Within a few years Faust's activities were circulating in translation in many European languages. In England they appeared somewhat amplified as *The Historie of the damnable life, and deserved death of Doctor John Faustus . . . translated into English by P. F. Gent.*, of which the earliest extant edition is dated 1592. This was the source from which Marlowe derived not only the structural pattern of his hero's career, but also Faustus's distinctive blend of character traits. The compiler of the *Faustbuch* and P. F. Gent. had already begun to transform the flashy, slightly shabby caster of horoscopes and befuddler of yokels from popular folklore into the Renaissance polymath of infinite ambition, and Marlowe continued this tendency by making his protagonist a figure of potential dignity and nobility of purpose, at least in the opening scenes of the play. Yet the cocky mountebank and illusionist are never far below the sober surface. Faustus is thus invested with a psychological ambiguity which contributes greatly to the human interest of the work that bears his name, and has encouraged actors to

attempt varied readings of the role on stage. At the same time, it
has been questioned whether Marlowe really makes Faustus a
coherent figure at all; can the twin facets of a dual personality
be made to harmonise?

Let us examine our initial impressions of Faustus. It is fitting
that we should first encounter a scholar in his study, though
some experts express doubts as to his true academic distinction,
finding errors of scholarship in his first speech. Some of these
may not have been intentional on Marlowe's part, but it seems
clear that, as Faustus engages in his session of self-analysis, he
is not presented uncritically. His examination of biblical texts
appears particularly perfunctory. In quoting scripture to
demonstrate not only the banality of theological studies but
also the bleakness of Christian doctrine, Faustus omits in both
instances clauses which mitigate the rigour of the primary
statements he reads out. He refers to the wages of sin being
death, but leaves out that 'the gift of God is eternal life'; he
quotes, 'If we say that we have no sin, we deceive ourselves, and
the truth is not in us', but 'If we confess our sins, he is faithful
and just to forgive us our sins' goes for nothing. This suggests
some deliberate wilfulness in ignoring that aspect of Christian
teaching which does not accord with his sceptical mood.
Faustus discounts the emphasis Christianity has usually placed
on the forgiveness of sins, a tenet he shortly demonstrates his
inability to accept. His later conviction of his own damnation
may indeed date from this point.

How should we respond to his rejection of humane studies for
the exploration of the occult? His dismissal of philosophical
enquiry with the remark that 'A greater subject fitteth Faustus'
wit' smacks of nothing worse than intellectual arrogance:
Nicholas Brooke might even regard it as manifesting heroic
confidence in mental gifts beyond the commonplace. But less
ambivalent is the comment which terminates Faustus's rejection of the physician's art:

> Yet art thou still but Faustus, and a man.
> Couldst thou make men to live eternally
> Or being dead raise them to life again,
> Then this profession were to be esteem'd.   [i 23–6]

The inference here must be that Faustus aspires to a condition transcending the viable boundaries of human attainment: he demands powers no mortal creature can acquire. Postulate a Christian universe, and a charge of blasphemy might be preferred, since Faustus is demanding for man what belongs only to God. Set aside the strongly Christian frame of reference and Faustus's request must still appear ridiculously presumptuous: he is asking the impossible. Yet, simultaneously, we can recognise (being human) the seductive promise to make its adherents superhuman which black magic holds out – 'A sound magician is a demi-god' – and the apparently limitless potential that arouses the excited neophyte to exclaim in quickened verse:

> O, what a world of profit and delight,
> Of power, of honour, of omnipotence,
> Is promis'd to the studious artisan!   [i 52–4]

How should we distinguish the legitimate ambition of genius as it seeks to leap over barriers imposed by arbitrary power or human limitations, from the vanity of a discontentment which so overwhelms the mind as to provoke demands full of reckless absurdity? Some words from Matthew Arnold's *Culture and Anarchy* (1869) may be helpful. Writing of the differing connotations of the term 'curiosity' in English and non-English usage Arnold says,

> A liberal and intelligent eagerness about the things of the mind may be meant by a foreigner when he speaks of curiosity, but with us the word always conveys a certain notion of frivolous and unedifying activity. . . . As there is a curiosity about intellectual matters which is futile, and merely a disease, so there is certainly a curiosity – a desire after things of the mind simply for their own sakes and for the pleasure of seeing them as they are, – which is, in an intelligent being, natural and laudable. Nay, and the very desire to see things as they are, implies a balance and regulation of mind which is not often attained without fruitful effort, and which is the very opposite of the blind and diseased impulse of mind which is what we mean to blame when we blame curiosity.

To assess Faustus's conduct aright we need to discriminate between these two definitions of 'curiosity'. It is true that his desire is partly after 'the things of the mind simply for their own sakes', and that this certainly forms one strand in the tapestry of speculations that Faustus weaves in lines 78–96. But, despite references to 'strange philosophies' and the resolution of ambiguities, despite the astronomical and geographical researches to come, Faustus's spirit of disinterested enquiry is undoubtedly adulterated by less worthy motives: the desire for personal kudos and wealth, for pomp and luxury, for sensual satisfaction. Alongside 'a liberal and intelligent eagerness about the things of the mind' lurk 'certain notions of frivolous and unedifying activity'. Furthermore, as E. D. Pendry observes in his Everyman edition of Marlowe, Faustus's catalogue of projects is too various and incoherent to be admired. It reveals a marked absence of Arnold's 'balance and regulation of mind'; Faustus strives not only 'to see things as they are' but also to see them as he would like them to be if he ruled the universe. Moreover, he not only lacks a clearly defined, single-track ambition; he also cherishes no proposal for benefiting mankind for which he is prepared to forfeit his soul. Instead, he has in his overloaded brain a series of flamboyantly unrelated desires which spill out like a stream of toys from Santa's sack. And Faustus, like a small child in a superstore, wants to possess them all, and all at once.

So it is not the whole truth to speak of Faustus as a man who trespasses beyond the permitted boundaries for the sake of the acquisition of pure knowledge. His reasons for opening negotiations with Lucifer are far from simple, and his fault in selling his soul may be seen today as that of a bored genius rather than of a wicked blasphemer, his undoing stemming less from sinful perversity than from a nature essentially trivial. Those who point to the element of vulgarity and meretriciousness in Faustus's make-up – an inability to distinguish what is of solid worth from what is tawdry – are perhaps closer to a true reading of his complex nature than those for whom he is either humanist saint or Christian sinner. Our own age offers plentiful examples of responsible and respected figures temporarily dazzled by the bright lights or the fat cheque into demeaning themselves in various ways, but we do not have to resort to modern instances to be aware of the nature of Faustus's temptation. Perhaps we should regard him as a would-be ascetic who has previously ignored his material and emotional needs, or as a teacher whose pursuit of academic excellence has

been less for the advancement of the subject than himself.
Faustus could be Marlowe's portrait of a poor scholar of
humble background whose learning has not brought him the
social and economic success he truly craves, forcing him to
select illicit routes to satisfaction. Certainly Faustus seeks
private glory and personal gain from the contract as well as
laudable and altruistic goals. Whatever the key, it is precisely
because his noble ideals are compromised by more dubious
desires that we identify with the hero in his plight much more
readily than if he were some dusty pedant obsessed with some
self-abnegating research-project. However distinguished his
mind, Faustus's mortal frailties are such as to secure him our
sympathy even as we deplore his false sense of values.

Faustus's subsequent development is consistent with our
initial sight of him. His first encounter with Mephostophilis in
Scene iii should give him sufficient warning of the erroneous
assumptions he is making, not least by belittling the anguished
tones in which Lucifer's gloomy agent describes his own sense
of deprivation in a realm without God, and ignoring the stern
rebuke administered when Faustus with crass jocularity waxes
facetious at the demon's discomfort. The doctor's boastful
presumptuousness is more terrible now than mere scholarly
conceit:

> What, is great Mephostophilis so passionate
> For being deprived of the joys of heaven?
> Learn thou of Faustus manly fortitude
> And scorn those joys thou never shalt possess.   [iii 85–8]

Dramatic irony could hardly be better illustrated: we shall
watch Faustus's 'manly fortitude' in action during his final
agonies! Indeed, Faustus's behaviour throughout Scene iii is
frightening in its blindly absurd overconfidence: unterrified by
the word 'damnation', regarding men's souls as 'trifles', he fails
to link his own attitudes with the 'aspiring pride and insolence'
Mephostophilis ascribes to Lucifer. Blandly admitting that he
has 'incurred eternal death, / By desperate thoughts against
Jove's deity' [iii 90–1], Faustus permits his blasé mood to
sustain him throughout the scene.

Yet this state of bragging euphoria is punctuated by periods
of self-doubt and unease. Faustus's reaction at these moments

offers some insight into his psychological condition. His first
reservations in Scene v are stifled by his belief that God has no
love for him; when '*Homo fuge*' appears on his arm after the
contract is signed, it is clear that any religious belief he may
retain centres on the punitive God he has contrived from those
incomplete quotations he read out in Scene i:

> *Homo fuge*! Whither should I fly?
> If unto God, he'll throw me down to hell.   [v 77–8]

Faustus clearly lacks the capacity to believe in a god of love or
in the viability of his own redemption. His conviction that
'Faustus' offence can ne'er be pardoned' [xix 41] has led
Pauline Honderich and others to suggest that through his hero
Marlowe illustrates the extreme Calvinist doctrine of predestination, which embodied the notion of a predetermined scheme
of election to salvation, and sets it against the more liberal
Catholic or Anglican dispensation that no repentant sinner is
beyond the reach of divine compassion. There is indeed a neat
verbal parallel between Faustus's cry in Scene vi, 'My heart is
harden'd, I cannot repent', and that of Bunyan's Man in the
Iron Cage in *The Pilgrim's Progress*: 'I have so hardened my
heart that I cannot repent.' When Faustus realises in Scene vi
that restraints are placed even on the Devil's apparently
infinite powers and calls on Christ for help, Lucifer's 'Christ
cannot save thy soul, for he is just' [vi 87] implies that he too
takes the same legalistic view of salvation as his intended
victim. Yet the text constantly indicates that Faustus is not so
damned as he thinks he is: for him the mercy which awaits the
falling sinner who calls to God betwixt stirrup and ground is
always available.

But Faustus does not simply fail to accept the notion of
forgiveness: he is terrorised by his diabolic masters into
shrinking from its effect on their treatment of him. Unlike the
Old Man of Scene xviii, Faustus is a physical coward, credible
enough in one who sets great store by bodily satisfactions, but
ironic in one who advises a demon to cultivate 'manly fortitude'
through his example. In Scene xviii, when Faustus is torn
between repentance and despair, Mephostophilis's threat to tear
his flesh is sufficiently lurid to cow him into submission, and for
him to repeat the words almost verbatim to his friends in Scene

xix. Yet the demon's reluctant response to Faustus's sadistic wish to watch the Old Man tormented points up the essential unimportance of any pain the devils can inflict on a resolute spirit.

However, in the last analysis it is less Faustus's lack of faith or his coward soul which ensures his defeat, but rather that basic lack of serious purpose already referred to, and the ease with which he can be diverted from both solid achievements and his own spiritual danger. Mephostophilis knows his man; as Faustus ponders the significance of the '*Homo fuge*' inscription, the demon's remedy is to hand: 'I'll fetch him somewhat to delight his mind' [v 82]. The hero himself feelingly catalogues in Scene vi the satisfactions which have allowed him not only to keep at bay despair and forestall thoughts of death but also to resolve never to repent and forgo such delicious experiences. But the clearest instance of the way Faustus blots out distasteful thoughts comes in his request for Helen,

> Whose sweet embraces may extinguish clear
> Those thoughts that do dissuade me from my vow,
> And keep mine oath I made to Lucifer.   [xviii 94–6]

Sexual desire and sycophancy combine to shut out the truth Faustus cannot face. It is precisely this love of 'vain pleasure', this need for constant stimulation and the avoidance of boredom, this inconsistent attitude to life's immense possibilities which connect the aspiring but easily distracted scholar with the boisterous prankster of the central scenes. Faustus's exotic travels, his disruptive antics at the papal court, the humiliation of Benvolio are as much part of his nature as the learned researches, his enjoyment of Homer's singing, his raptures over Helen of Troy: the combination reveals the restlessness of a personality ill-disciplined but common enough. If this is agreed, then the 'two Faustuses' of many analyses are one, albeit one with that schizophrenic temperament not unknown in academic circles. Readers of C. P. Snow's *Strangers and Brothers* may recall Roy Calvert, a brilliant scholar given to bouts of melancholia culminating in manic outbursts.

It has sometimes been claimed that Marlowe supplies insufficient data to compose a satisfactory character-portrait of Faustus, that many phases in his downfall are closed to us, and it is certainly true that no Elizabethan play can offer us the gradual psychological revelations we expect from a late Victorian or early modern novel. But, within its conventions, *Doctor Faustus* can convince us that credible human motives lie behind its protagonist's behaviour, even if they have to be inferred from time to time. For his personal character we can construct a plausible rationale, and, because we share with Faustus common failings, contradictions and incongruities, those qualities which make for what Pope called 'an April weather in the mind', we identify with him in both his foolish presumption and his fearful punishment.

4 'THE FORM OF FAUSTUS' FORTUNES'

'Our native Muse', wrote W. H. Auden in *The Sea and the Mirror* (while still an Englishman), 'is not exclusive. . . . No timid segregation by rank or taste for her.' These words remind us that, whatever virtues they exhibit, and they are legendary, the great plays of Shakespeare's time, by comparison with those of Pericles's Athens or Richelieu's France, often lack streamlined aesthetic structure, or stringent artistic control. Clowns brush shoulders with kings; high tragedy gives place to low farce; leading characters depart never to return; verse and prose nestle cheek by jowl; unrelated plots run concurrently; time and place prove elastic as the action swivels from Egypt to Rome and back, or Time as Chorus enters to persuade us that sixteen years have slid by. Foreign and classical example could rarely coax the exuberant yet unruly British colt into the paddock of ordered formality where it could be trained along more disciplined lines. Plays, such as *Gorboduc*, which adhered fairly strictly to regular rules failed to constitute acceptable models for those striving to satisfy the popular tastes of Elizabethan London.

Marlowe was the natural heir to the mixed traditions of the British stage. By the time he saw his *Tamburlaine* presented in the winter of 1587–8, the Elizabethan theatrical revolution was under way, and a medley of hybrid concoctions was being

served to those who swarmed daily to Shoreditch and the
Bankside to sample the exciting new fare. Such pieces as
survive indicate that few of those writing for the public
playhouses were greatly enamoured of the formal principles of
classical dramaturgy. Despite his university background, Marlowe was not ambitious to associate with those small esoteric
circles of writers solemnly attempting to imitate classical and
neoclassical tragedies which adhered with chaste fidelity to the
unities of time, place and action, but which were almost totally
devoid of warm, vibrant theatrical life. He threw in his lot with
men who were working to create great drama from different
conventions and based on different principles.

The authorship of *Faustus* is controversial, but the main
arguments do not involve those portions of the B-text allocated
to the combined pens of Rowley and Birde. In the B-text,
following Jump's numbering, Marlowe's hand is most
obviously detectable in the Prologue, the first seven scenes,
Chorus 1, the last three scenes, and the Epilogue. Whether
Marlowe or Rowley–Birde wrote the scene in which the
Scholars discover Faustus's body is unimportant, nor do we
need to debate whether or not Marlowe's probable collaborator
was solely responsible for Scenes iv and vi. The vital issue is
that of dramatic integrity. How far is *Faustus* a unified if
unharmonious whole, how far a series of heterogeneous
incidents linked by a common protagonist?

We must not do Marlowe the injustice of assuming that, had
we the complete text of the play that the public first saw in
1592–3, we should automatically receive the impression that he
lacked system. From the scenes which remain from that
original version, we can infer that he had worked out a coherent
pattern for its development, based on the juxtaposition of
scenes high in dramatic tension with those in which comedy or
farce predominate, possibly on the analogy of the moral
interludes. So after the seriousness of the hero's apostasy in
Scene i we relax with Wagner and the Scholars; after the
summoning of Mephostophilis to be Faustus's servant comes
Scene iv, in which Wagner binds Robin to serve *him*, and, if
Greg is right, a comic episode depicting Robin taking service at
an inn as ostler (and possibly taking an oath of apprenticeship)
may have followed Scene v. The incident in which Robin reads

to Dick from a book stolen from Faustus succeeds to that in which the doctor is diverted from his intention of repenting by Mephostophilis and the masque of the Seven Deadly Sins. In other words, dramatic structure, at least in the early part of *Faustus*, seems determined partly by a series of alternating contrasts, though it would be unduly flattering to suggest that the adventures of Robin, Dick and the yokels constitute anything as grand as a subplot. They mainly act as comic diversion of a fairly conventional type, but it may not be over-ingenious to suggest that they parody the exploits of Faustus in the drama's 'serious' phases. However, the main conclusion is that, where Marlowe seems certain to have had a hand in the action, an intelligible schéme can be detected.

It is harder to trace any very clear plan in the middle scenes, difficult to avoid Pendry's claim that in them 'Marlowe as much as Faustus . . . has lost a clear sense of what he is doing'. It is too easy to take refuge in the defence that Marlowe had no say in the scenes that intervene between Chorus 1 in Jump's text and Scene xviii, or to state that he simply left them to his collaborator's initiative. One suspects that Marlowe retained control of the central part of the original play, even if he did not compose every word of it, and that therefore his conception of the function of those scenes has a bearing on their content, even when Rowley and Birde came to revise and add to the text as it existed in 1602.

Can we discover what Marlowe had in mind? Evidence has already been put forward to demonstrate that Faustus himself is less of a split personality than has often been claimed, that the aspiring academic and the jesting conjuror are features of the same temperament. Moreover, we need to remind ourselves of Marlowe's constant fondness for irony and paradox, which led him elsewhere to present in close juxtaposition the most heroic sentiments and the most squalid actions man was capable of: the majesty and cruelty of Tamburlaine; the intellectual grasp and malice of Barabas; the tenderness of Edward's love for Gaveston and the vindictive obscenity of his murder. That Marlowe set no store by arbitrary decorum either is illustrated by the slightly embarrassed remarks of Richard Jones, when publishing *Tamburlaine* in 1590:

I have (purposely) omitted and left out some fond and frivolous
Jestures, digressing (and in my poore opinion) far unmeet for the
matter, which I thought, might seeme more tedious unto the wise,
than any way els to be regarded, though (happily) they have bene of
some vaine conceited fondlings greatly gaped at, what times they
were shewed upon the stage in their graced deformities: nevertheless now, to be mixtured in print with such matter of worth, it wuld
proove a great disgrace to so honorable and stately a historie. . . .

Such remarks may caution those who hope to assign to
Marlowe simply the lofty and 'poetic' passages which help to
make up the variegated texture of *Doctor Faustus*.

We can perhaps approach the central episodes in a more
liberal spirit than Richard Jones's, and treat them as part of the
drama rather than as irrelevant or distracting. What lies before
us is after all a complete play, not merely a set of poetic 'gems'
which we have to carve from the contextual rock in which they
are embedded. While some still subscribe to the view that all is
dross that is not Christopher's, the present writer like others
takes the view that *Faustus* possesses more dramatic unity than
is often recognised, given the generous standards of the
Elizabethan stage in such matters.

What can be said in defence of Scenes viii–xvii as contri-
butions to the total effect? Marlowe's technical problem was
undoubtedly to fill the time elapsing between the moment that
Faustus signs the contract in blood, and his terrible last night
on earth. While his source offered him a plethora of incidents, it
suggested no continuous theme linking the initial pledge to the
ultimate hour of retribution. Cosmic exploration could hardly
be staged effectively (a fact Nicholas Brooke feels places undue
emphasis on the presumed triviality of Faustus's pranks);
extended conversations with Mephostophilis could become
static; too many crises of conscience would be monotonous; the
apparition of Helen had to be held back for the penultimate
crisis of the action. Marlowe was thus faced with a difficulty
shared by authors of detective stories as well as by the author
of *Hamlet*: how could he sustain the interest without moving too
swiftly to the final crescendo?

The uncharitable answer would be that he could not.
However, what Marlowe attempted was to utilise four episodes
from P. F.'s *Damnable Life*, and weave these loosely into a

sequence to supply his play with its core. But the episodes clearly have a dramatic purpose. Even if we reject the idea that his achievements in the central scenes justify the impiety of Faustus's bargain, they do reveal facets of his personality not incompatible with what we have seen before, but now far more blatant. All the incidents demonstrate a streak of spitefulness, an urge to humiliate and score off others, very much in keeping with the cruelty displayed by the demonic fraternity towards him. His vindictiveness may also assist us to recognise a certain poetic justice in the inexorable harshness of Faustus's own punishment.

Structurally regarded, the scenes in question offer a respite from the intense emotions stirred up by the discovery of what Faustus has ventured upon, even lulling us into a false sense of assurance that 'Faustus may repent and save his soul'. In a physical sense, too, they act as a transitional phase in the action whereby we leave the narrow confines of Faustus's study – the prison of his spirit, if we choose to interpret his bargain as liberating him – and embark with him on a tour of the world of action and affairs beyond the scholar's ivory tower. For some observers considerable importance attaches to the strong contrast which Faustus's apparently insignificant achievements offer to what he might have hoped to attain. Even those who argue that the 'trivial' exploits are not all Faustus succeeds in accomplishing or who argue that an Elizabethan audience would have been impressed by his spectacular attainments must as a result view the central episodes as relevant to the play as a whole.

Since the scene- and act-divisions of modern editions appear in neither the A- nor the B-text, it is impossible to establish whether or nor Marlowe was guided in building his structural framework by the example of the so-called 'five-act structure' of classical antiquity. Some uncertainty remains as to whether those who wrote for the Elizabethan public theatres thought consciously in terms of act-divisions, or if they achieved their formal patterns through natural instinct and coincidence. But there is no doubt that many Elizabethan plays do divide very satisfactorily into five acts, and, like most of Shakespeare's works, *Doctor Faustus* in the B-version separates into five distinct phases corresponding closely to the classical scheme. Act I might thus contain the first four scenes, Act II the next three, Act III Scenes viii–x, Act IV Scenes xi–xvii, while the final three make up Act V. The fact that such a system would assign separate acts to Faustus's traffic with the Devil, the bargain and its aftermath, the intrusion at the Vatican, the escapades at the courts of Charles V and the Duke of Vanholt, and the final *dénouement*, appears to be further evidence that *Faustus* is far from being an uncontrolled muddle, and that within the broad criteria governing the shape of Elizabethan plays it has more than sufficient structural integrity.

5 'Heavenly Words'

Amid the excitement engendered by the present-day emphasis on Elizabethan plays as scripts intended for theatrical performance, we must never forget that most are largely written in verse, and that it is still essential to treat them as dramatic poems too. As highly wrought, highly complex linguistic organisms, they require far closer attention than if they were entirely couched in the naturalistic speech of everyday urban life.

Whatever we may decide that poetry is – Dr Johnson thought it was easier to say what poetry was *not* – the fact that it is generally agreed to be language under certain kinds of pressure, language deployed in certain special ways to produce heightened effects, makes it a very suitable medium for drama, or at least for drama of a particular kind. Poetry seems entirely appropriate to the characters Marlowe created, and to their situations. Heightened characters with a heightened imaginative awareness of life's potential do not sound pretentious when they conjure up the exotic, the infinite, the unattainable. Their natural mode of expression is a diction rich in simile and metaphor, drenched in high-sounding comparisons and lofty epithets; they unselfconsciously employ 'images of the sun, moon and stars, of meteors and storms, of distant places, of precious stones and metals, of legendary and mythological doings' (Pendry, Everyman edn, p. vii).

Yet we should be wary of detaching their words from the dramatic situation that called them forth. In Marlowe's early works, in *Dido Queen of Carthage* and *Tamburlaine*, one can extract large sections of the play from their immediate context and expose them as no more than passages of narrative verse which contribute nothing to enhance the theatrical moment. In *Faustus* poetic language has been successfully assimilated to dramatic ends. Though Marlowe certainly wrote poetry before he wrote poetic plays, he had to learn that the demands of drama are different from those of lyric or epic before plays like *Faustus* could result. With this in mind, we may now examine four samples of Marlowe's dramatic poetry.

1. The first movement of Faustus's initial soliloquy [i 1–62] runs to line 47 before its argument is substantially developed, but it is divided into four shorter units. In each case Faustus takes a 'specimen' from writings on the major disciplines of the medieval curriculum in the form of one or more relevant Latin maxims. He reflects briefly on each, always concluding that the subject is to be rejected *in toto* because of what he finds unsatisfactory in the selected 'specimen'. The inadequacy of this as a scholarly method has been shown with reference to 'Jerome's Bible' (p. 25), but, rhetorically speaking, it suggests that Faustus's successive curt 'farewells' are stepping-stones by which the orator can attain to his true theme, a eulogy in favour of magic. While at line 6 it was 'Sweet Analytics' that had 'ravish'd' him, at line 109, where the line is purposefully echoed, the cause is now 'magic, magic'. Faustus's diction in reviewing his orthodox studies abounds in finite images: 'Settle thy studies'; 'sound the depth'; 'level at the end': indeed, the very word 'end' itself (carrying of course another doom-laden sense in this play) occurs five times between lines 4 and 18. Deciding that he confronts a series of *culs-de-sac*, Faustus reaches beyond to a world apparently brimming with limitless possibilities, and his imagery too is released from bondage. The 'quiet poles' are invoked, winds are raised, clouds rent, but, compared with the specific but uncompromising statements found in his previous analyses, what Faustus meditates on now is nothing more than a set of exciting but vague uncertainties stretching 'as far as doth the mind of man'

but without concrete identity. The weighty polysyllables which succeed the rejection of the harshness of divinity convey the impressive appeal of necromancy, but Marlowe's choice of 'heavenly' as a descriptive epithet provides another deliberate touch of irony:

> These metaphysics of magicians
> And necromantic books are heavenly   [48–9]

2. Irony dominates Faustus's first conversation with Mephostophilis in iii 37–103. The pattern of their exchanges is dictated by a sequence of questions from the doctor, to which the demon returns dusty answers filled with significance, had Faustus the perceptive humility to take advantage of hints. Paradoxically, the first query is the demon's own, but Faustus's grandiose 'charge' that Mephostophilis should carry out his behests –

> Be it to make the moon drop from her sphere
> Or the ocean to overwhelm the world   [40–1]

– bears within it intimations of disaster on a cosmic scale. Moreover, his bland assumption of control is challenged by Mephostophilis's response that Lucifer's prior permission is needed before any demon can serve a human master. The scholar's 'whatever Faustus shall command' is firmly snubbed by the echoic 'No more than he commands must we perform' [44].

More wind is taken out of Faustus's sails by what follows: his queries as to his own status in the hellish scheme of things indicate an eager desire to retain his belief in magic and the authority it gives him. His pretensions are deflated in almost comic retorts:

> FAU.   Did not he charge thee to appear to me?
> MEPH.   No, I came hither of mine own accord.   [45–6]

Similarly the demon makes short work of the notion that it was Faustus's conjuring that forced him to manifest himself: he has come to 'get his glorious soul', the adjective conveying the sense of 'vain-glorious' or 'presumptuous'. All that mumbo-jumbo wasn't needed, says he dismissively: 'the shortest cut for conjuring' is to forswear the Christian god and pray to Lucifer. Painfully anxious to persuade his visitor of his true allegiance, in lines 57–63 Faustus puts on a show of bravado, the allusions to 'Elysium' and 'the old philosophers' suggesting that he sees himself as a latter-day pagan, the inheritor of the old classical spirit of Stoicism, ironic in a man who will later whimper on the verge of Hell.

There follows one of the most riveting passages in the play: Faustus's teasing and idly curious questions as he probes into Lucifer's antecedents and the nature of damnation are met by Mephostophilis's replies, dignified, courteous, terse: two single lines, then a couplet, then a triplet. Yet after a reluctant response to the casual 'Where are you damn'd?' there comes a great outburst of pained remonstrance which dispels the tension, starting with a line of magnificent monosyllables – 'Why, this is hell, nor am I out of it' [78] – which annihilates Faustus's donnishly clever-clever question preceding it. The doctor's self-consciously daring reply to this anguished out-burst, flippantly dismissing 'eternal death' as inconsequential and increasing the tempo as the idea of 'living in all voluptu-ousness' takes hold, makes little impression beside the dread sense of deprivation evoked through the charged power of Mephostophilis's conventional religious imagery:

> Think'st thou that I, who saw the face of God,
> And tasted the eternal joys of heaven,
> Am nor tormented with ten thousand hells
> In being depriv'd of everlasting bliss?   [79–82]

3. The lines to Helen (xviii 99–118) are in little need of laboured diagnosis: they constitute pure theatre poetry in which the evocative power of the verse is perfectly wedded to a visible form present on stage. From the opening line with its elaborate pattern of sibilants suggesting the hushed awe of the watching devotee, not daring to allow a harsh sound to pass his lips, to the second with its hard dental consonants as he moves to Helen's destructive potential, to line 3 with its dreamy 'make me immortal' culminating in the hard 'k' of 'kiss' echoed by 'suck' in the next the entire speech illustrates the variety and pliability of Marlowe's blank verse at its best. The word 'sweet' by which Faustus addresses Helen occurs throughout the play as a term of approbation, appropriate to a man whose main

object in life often seems to be pleasure, and who shrinks from
the harsh and the unpalatable.

The artistry of the speech is remarkable, but the dramatic
context is important too. Helen's role – demon or not – is to lure
Faustus away from thoughts of repentance. Hence the imagery
associated with her presence should not be admired for its
verbal beauty alone, but also for indicating the nature of a
theatrical situation. The language throughout is that of
deception and destruction: the siege of Troy occasioned by
Paris's abduction of the married Helen; the burning of the
Trojan citadel; the shameful killing of Achilles; the partisan-
ship of the pagan gods. Even the allusion to Jupiter recalls the
incineration of the presumptuous Semele when she demanded
to see the god in his Olympian form. 'Hapless' Semele played
with divine fire; even Arethusa is stigmatised as 'wanton':
Faustus resembles them both, and Helen will draw him to
destruction as utterly as she did the Trojans.

4. Wolfgang Clemen in *English Tragedy before Shakespeare* (1955;
trs. 1961) observes how the hero's soliloquies 'are the natural
vehicle for the expression of the spiritual warfare and the
conflicts of ideas that take place in Faustus himself' (p. 148),
and nowhere is this more true than in his closing speech in
Scene xix. The tension created by the clash between the
speaker's certitude of his own fate and the desperate hope that
he may somehow evade it is reflected in his nervous, shifting,
hysterical tone as he toys with and discards one possible
escape-route after another. Again, this is dramatic poetry
precisely attuned to a stage situation: Faustus's tormented
mind is not presented in a vacuum, but as that of a man who, as
he looks at the starlit sky, the clouds, the earth at his feet, is
reminded at every turn of his doomed state. As Clemen notes,
'the spiritual conflict is transformed into something that
happens before our eyes' (p. 153). Religious concepts take on
physical existence: Christ's blood does stream in the firma-
ment; God does stretch out his arm; the soul takes on form as
Faustus cries for it to be changed 'into little water drops, / And
fall into the ocean' [185–6].

The execution of the passage is superb: the broken lines
occurring throughout offer scope for dramatic pauses; the

frequent repetitions of single words underline the emotional
pressure; above all, the insistent use of monosyllables reinforces
the sense of tragic doom, commencing with 'Now hast thou but
one bare hour to live' [134], which, like the remorseless ticking
of the clock, picks off the last sixty minutes of Faustus's mortal
existence. All the most telling sentences in the speech are
monosyllabic: 'Oh, I'll leap up to my God!', 'One drop would
save my soul, half a drop. Ah, my Christ!' and, most terribly,
'My God, my God! Look not so fierce on me!' Equally
remarkable is the accelerating cadence which has only two
single disyllables (the names of hero and villain) to disrupt the
heavy beat of lone words:

> The stars move still, time runs, the clock will strike,
> The devil will come, and Faustus must be damn'd.   [143–4]

Again the versatility which Marlowe displays in handling the
blank-verse unit is astounding. To convey in fifty-eight lines the
impression of an hour passing is masterly, but he also succeeds
in making us believe that a whole hour's worth of thoughts have
travelled through his hero's mind, as it flutters from vain hope
to vain hope in panic. To exploit the potential of his medium to
the full, Marlowe had to produce a virtuoso performance, yet
he rarely deviates from the normal decasyllabic line, except to
interpolate short lines of two, three, or four syllables, and to
fashion two memorable Alexandrine lines which add to the
sense of infinite yearning:

> See, see where Christ's blood streams in the firmament!
> One drop would save my soul, half a drop. Ah, my Christ!
> [146–7]

Marlowe is highly inventive too in varying the position of the
natural pause or caesura within the line. Since blank verse was
still in its relative infancy in Britain, the tendency was to allow
the break to fall with monotonous regularity at the middle and
end of each individual line. Marlowe's capacity to handle the
form so that the pauses occur in a whole range of positions, and
his ability to run one line on into the next, are not merely feats of
accomplished poetic technique. In Faustus's last speech they
contribute profoundly to the portrait of a human being at the
end of his tether, converting the rather stiff rhetorical device of

dramatic soliloquy into an intensely powerful expression of personal anguish.

6 'What Means This Show?'

By now it is established that a playtext as printed is merely the blueprint for a stage presentation, which demands of us the capacity to recreate theatrical impact from the hints supplied. It is not enough to read the words; we have to hear them spoken in our imagination. Stage directions have to be translated into a setting with doors and windows, or trees and benches, that we can visualise. We have to think how people are to be grouped on stage, or what the impact of an exit or an entrance will be; we have to realise how movement or gesture or lighting-effects can colour the way remarks are delivered or reacted to. In brief, we have to direct the play in our own heads, complete with set, costumes, lights, music and so forth, before we can truly say that we are 'reading' a play. Such ability has to be cultivated, especially if we do not often get the chance to watch drama in performance.

Despite all the specialised satisfaction it now gives, the drama of the Elizabethan age was a genuinely popular form of entertainment to which all classes of society, all levels of brow, were irresistibly attracted. And *Faustus* we know was one of the most successful plays of its time. A graphic impression of its earliest presentations is found in Sir John Melton's *Astrologaster: or the Figure-Caster* of 1620: 'shagge-hayr'd Devills runne roaring over the Stage with Squibs in their mouthes, while Drummers make Thunder in the Tyring-house, and the twelve-penny Hirelings [i.e. stage-hands] make artificiall Lightning in their Heavens'. Such an impact did the devils in *Faustus* make that it was freely rumoured among the superstitious that actual demons had been known to participate in the action!

Marlowe's play still offers scope for spectacle and sensational effects: the diabolic crew who present Faustus with crowns and rich apparel, serve food and toss fire-crackers; the parade of

Deadly Sins; the papal banquet and the imperial masque; the false head and the detachable leg – all contribute colour, movement, and grotesque humour to the performance. But these are merely the more showy aspects of a piece abounding in far subtler effects. Space does not permit us to subject the whole play to close analysis, but a selection of instances may serve to indicate what we can glean from the attempt to bring a playtext to life.

The opening scene with Faustus alone on the stage may seem static enough by contrast with what follows, but it focuses immediate attention on the solitary burner of the midnight oil, suggesting that this is the tragedy of an individual, rather than one which involves an entire community. Such an introduction pinpoints Faustus's introspective, self-absorbed nature, and it is curious that for most of the play Faustus rarely makes close contact with any other character apart from Mephostophilis. His encounters with the Emperor and the Duke of Vanholt are formalised exchanges of compliments. It is a surprise in Scene xviii when he turns out to have friends who care for his welfare; generally Faustus remains adrift in the sea of his own egotism.

The presence of the Good and Bad Angels is a device from the morality tradition which theatricalises the hero's moral conflict in an old-fashioned but highly visual manner, whether or not satire is the aim. Their appearance like that of the devils in Scenes iii and xix provides a dimension easily forgotten while reading: Faustus's drama involves him not simply with the terrestrial world but with the entire cosmos, a truth reinforced by the scene of his collapse where he stands physically and spiritually suspended between Heaven and Hell, while the forces of darkness muster in the wings. At all times drama comprises a visual as well as a verbal element.

One of the most striking moments in the play is provided by the Seven Deadly Sins, yet it is hard to avoid the feeling when reading that this 'pastime' is little more than an uneasily interpolated diversion. However, in the theatre its presence not only relieves the tensions of the previous scenes, but also helps to foreshadow the tawdry aspect of some of Faustus's exploits; the Sins typify the pseudo-glamorous exterior of Lucifer's gift. That Faustus expresses himself 'delighted' by this farrago of satirically conceived grotesques tells us a good deal about his

own tastes (whether or not he is trying to ingratiate himself
with Lucifer) and serves as a foretaste of slick trickery and petty
spitefulness to come.

   Scenes which scholars feel confident that Marlowe had no
hand in writing (viii–xvii in Jump's edition) constitute the
more conventionally spectacular parts of the play with the
ceremonial procession and banquet at the Vatican, the
excommunication ritual and the interlude of Alexander, and
the 'battle scene' which closes Scene xiii of the B-text. Much of
this appears to be introduced to keep the less thoughtful part of
the audience happy, but not everything in the central scenes
anticipates Cecil B. De Mille. Some of the pleasure of the action
depends on such age-old staging-devices as disguises and
impersonation, as when Faustus and Mephostophilis dress as
cardinals and succeed in rescuing Bruno from the clutches of
the Papacy. Vigorous physical action occurs when the Holy
Father ascends his throne by way of Bruno's back (a device
Marlowe had already employed in *Tamburlaine*), when the
invisible scholar snatches away the choicest dishes, or when the
Horse-Courser pulls off Faustus's leg. Dramatic irony is found,
too, when the Pope is heard wishing that the Doctor's soul
might be damned for ever for his irreverence, and the Friars
pronounce a curse upon him. The tone may be comic and the
Roman Catholic faith mocked, but an underlying note of
warning is also struck. The Emperor's court scenes include
some farce, but they are also filled with the spirit of magical
entertainment at which Faustus excels, and our support for him
against Benvolio is partly a reflection of his success as a
conjuror, however temporary our allegiance may be. We are
visually impressed by the apparition of Alexander and his
train, and, even if we cannot taste the Duchess's grapes, we can
at least see them and savour the joy they bring. Thus the
theatrical frame of reference retains an importance in governing our response to Faustus the showman as well as Faustus the
scholar.

   The theatrical quality of the final scenes requires little
analysis. The first sight of Helen has been adversely criticised
as weakening her major appearance to Faustus later, but it
supplies the hero with a motive for requesting her as mistress, as
well as whetting the spectators' appetites for her return in a

manner which enables them to share Faustus's raptures at her beauty. Neither the warning of the Old Man nor Faustus's brief flirtation with the idea of suicide are novel, the incident in which the hero is tempted to dispatch himself with a dagger being directly adapted from morality plays of the previous age, but again they provide graphic stage images of mental and emotional situations. Though the Old Man is conceived as a human character rather than a symbolic one, he adopts something of the abstract function of the Good and Bad Angels, as Greg points out. His defiance of the forces of evil at the end of Scene xviii acts as a memorable contrast to the ensuing defeat of Faustus at their hands at the end of the scene which immediately follows.

Scene xix was probably the most powerful and moving episode ever staged in the English theatre up to that point, Shakespeare's *Richard III* notwithstanding. While the devils watch from above (probably a Rowley–Birde addition, though it could have featured in Marlowe's original), Faustus is shorn first of his earthly friends and then (in another addition) of his spiritual guardian; once more he is alone on the stage as he was at the start, but now the comfortable furnishings of his study have gone. He stands naked and vulnerable between open sky and bare earth. After the prose scene with the scholars and its more matter-of-fact register, the colossal power of Marlowe's writing fuses with the image of a single figure alone on a bare platform, restlessly pacing about, calling on the universe to stop still that time may cease. As the tension builds, words and actions are perfectly matched, while the spectators strain their ears to catch the first notes of the bell which tolls for Faustus's doom. Although another scene which may be Marlowe's follows in the B-text, it is the stage picture of a man vainly attempting to evade his destiny which remains with us at the close of the drama.

PART TWO: PERFORMANCE

7 INTRODUCTION

The following four productions have been selected for special consideration in this section:

1. The Old Vic Theatre Company's presentation at the Assembly Hall, Edinburgh, on 22 August 1961, restaged at the Old Vic Theatre, London on 14 September 1961; director: Michael Benthall; *Faustus*: Paul Daneman; *Mephostophilis*: Michael Goodliffe; *Lucifer*: Robert Eddison; *Chorus*: Walter Hudd; designer: Michael Annals.

2. The RSC production at the Memorial Theatre, Stratford-upon-Avon, on 27 June 1968; director: Clifford Williams; *Faustus*: Eric Porter; *Mephostophilis*: Terrence Hardiman; *Chorus*: Clifford Rose; designer: Abd' Elkader Farrah.

3. The RSC presentation at the Lyceum Theatre, Edinburgh, on 26 August 1974, and at the Aldwych Theatre, London, 5 September 1974; director: John Barton; *Faustus*: Ian McKellen; *Mephostophilis*: Emrys Jones; *Lucifer*: Clement McCallin; designer: Michael Annals.

4. A production at the Lyric Studio, Hammersmith, on 25 February 1980, restaged at the Fortune Theatre, London, on 27 March 1980; director: Christopher Fettes; *Faustus*: James Aubrey; *Mephostophilis*: Patrick Magee; *Beelzebub/Pope*: David Rappaport; designer: Kandis Cook.

The history of Marlowe's *Faustus* in the modern theatre begins on 2 July 1896. On that date William Poel, passionate advocate of a return to Elizabethan-style auditoria and staging-methods for drama of that period, revived the play in St George's Hall, Langham Place, London, employing a set-up reproducing as far as possible details given in the contract for constructing the

Fortune playhouse in January 1600. Poel's presentation, seen again on 4 July 1896 and revived with a fresh cast in the autumn of 1904, was deliberate and responsible, as self-conscious as any pioneering revival of a venerable antique was bound to be, but a positive and loving gesture towards a neglected classic, none the less.

However, reservations about the stageworthiness of non-Shakespearean Elizabethan plays in general was doubtless responsible for the unwillingness of most professional companies to risk their reputations by staging Marlowe's tragedy prior to the Second World War. Only amateur or specialist groups seemed prepared to venture. On 25 and 26 October 1925 the Phoenix Society, a 'private' organisation dedicated to reviving Elizabethan and Restoration plays, presented *Faustus* at London's New Oxford Theatre with Ion Swinley in the lead. Again, an approximation to an Elizabethan stage-setting encouraged stylisation and intimacy, with the accent placed on swiftness of speech and continuity of action. Nevertheless, it was generally felt that Allan Wade's production, which included fewer cuts than Poel's, exposed an innate textual dichotomy between stirring poetry and what many agreed to be piffling stupidity.

The next noteworthy presentation was given a more medieval orientation. On 20 August 1929 Nugent Monck (who played Robin for Poel in 1904) directed the Maddermarket Players from Norwich in a production mounted in the Chapter House of Canterbury Cathedral as part of the first Canterbury Festival. *Faustus* formed a double bill with *Everyman*, a morality drama some eighty years its senior, and the theme of the earlier work influenced the manner in which the Elizabethan piece was interpreted. Drastic editing, a quasi-ecclesiastical venue, Monck's temperamental melancholy and his declared preference for 'a maximum of taste and the minimum of vulgarity' combined to convert Marlowe's distinctly mongrel tragedy into an austere discourse on the wages of sin in which ambivalences and ironies disappeared in order to offer spectators a complementary counterpart to the salvation of Everyman.

Heavy cutting was also a feature of the first modern commercial presentation. On 8 January 1937 Orson Welles and John Houseman produced *Faustus* at the Maxine Elliott

Theater, New York, with Welles himself in the lead. Unlike Monck, whose effects were of the simplest, Welles deployed a wide range of technical devices to restore to the action those kinds of visual excitement through which the play had stimulated its earliest audiences. Despite a strong element of eclecticism, this production succeeded in attracting much attention in its own right, rather than as an antiquarian curiosity: Welles undoubtedly brought the play's impact home to non-specialist spectators. Yet whether a production which omits large chunks of the extant text solves satisfactorily the difficulties of staging Marlowe's tragedy in the modern theatre must occupy us later.

Professional presentations followed at the Rudolf Steiner Hall, London, on 12 March 1940, and at the Liverpool Playhouse, where the Old Vic Company was in residence, on 16 May 1944, but it was a post-war production which next commanded major critical attention. On 12 July 1946 Walter Hudd's version of *Faustus* opened at the Shakespeare Memorial Theatre, Stratford-upon-Avon, with Robert Harris in the lead and Hugh Griffith as Mephostophilis. Hudd's directorial inventiveness and Harris's speaking of the verse were admired, though the latter's portrayal of the exalted, scholarly romantic glossed over less commendable traits in the Doctor's character. At the revival of 9 April 1947 Paul Scofield replaced Hugh Griffith.

The Old Vic Company ventured for a second time at the New Theatre, London, on 7 October 1948, but the direction by John Burrell was generally no more to the critics' liking than was the Faustus of Sir Cedric Hardwicke. This distinguished actor, essaying a 'modern' restrained reading, lost the impassioned vitality and the poetic ardour of a scholar eager for satisfaction, and not for the last occasion Faustus was overshadowed by his Mephostophilis, in this instance Robert Eddison, 'a commanding figure full of beautifully-spoken ethereal authority' according to the *Daily Herald* for 8 October. Whether or not these qualities are truly appropriate to Mephostophilis, the 1948 Old Vic production highlights the importance of getting the balance between Doctor and demon correctly adjusted.

Neither the Old Vic nor the Stratford version of *Faustus*

1. Faustus (Robert Harris) and Mephostophilis (Hugh Griffith) confront the Deadly Sins in Walter Hudd's production at the Shakespeare Memorial Theatre, Stratford, 12 July 1946. © Angus McBean photograph, Harvard Theatre Collection.

2. Faustus (Paul Daneman) and Mephostophilis (Michael Goodliffe) at the Papal Court, in Michael Benthall's Old Vic production, 22 August 1961, first performed at the Edinburgh Festival. Courtesy of the Edinburgh Festival Organisation.

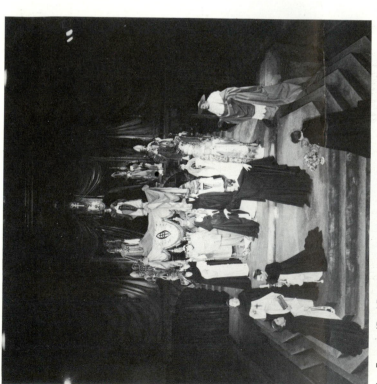

3. Maggie Wright as Helen and Eric Porter as Faustus in Clifford Williams's RSC production at the Shakespeare Memorial Theatre, Stratford, 27 June 1968. © Philip Stearns, courtesy of the BBC Hulton Picture Library.

4. Faustus (Eric Porter) menaced by the Seven Deadly Sins in Clifford Williams's RSC production, 27 June 1968. © Douglas Jeffrey, courtesy of the *Illustrated London News* Picture Library.

5. Faustus (Ian McKellen) and the Good Angel, in John Barton's RSC production at the Lyceum Theatre, Edinburgh, 26 August 1974. © Donald Cooper.

6. Beelzebub (David Rappaport) and Mephostophilis (Patrick Magee) in Christopher Fettes's production at the Lyric Studio, Hammersmith, 25 February 1980. © *Sunday Times.*

sparked off a spate of revivals in the 1950s; the next significant performance came in March 1957, when an Oxford don, Nevill Coghill, directed the work for the Oxford University Dramatic Society, attempting to bring out the paradoxes in Faustus's psychology. Coghill returned to the play in February 1966, when his guest players were the renowned Hollywood stars Richard Burton and Elizabeth Taylor; in a version later filmed, Burton determinedly underplayed the Doctor in an unromantic interpretation somewhat at odds with the resonant lines in which the character expresses himself. Once more it was Mephostophilis, played by Andreas Teuber, a student, who won much of the critical acclaim, while Burton's Faustus was found disappointing.

Between Coghill's twin productions another professional presentation had taken place. On 22 August 1961 Michael Benthall directed the play for the Old Vic at the Assembly Hall, Edinburgh, transferring the production to the Old Vic Theatre on 14 September. Faustus was played as a youthful don by Paul Daneman, while Mephostophilis was Michael Goodliffe, Robert Eddison having graduated to the part of Lucifer. The production was visually most impressive, especially at Edinburgh, where spectators sat on three sides of a projecting platform: the return to the then more customary proscenium stage of the Old Vic drew adverse comment, the *Daily Telegraph* reviewer decreeing that *Faustus* could 'no longer survive conventional production', as if it already had many conventional presentations to its name!

Clifford Williams's version of the play for the Royal Shakespeare Company at Stratford on 27 June 1968 had traditional features as well as more unusual ones, including the quite needlessly notorious 'nude Helen of Troy' episode. Williams, like Coghill, tried to do justice to all the varied aspects of Faustus's personality, but failed to weld them into a unified character that Eric Porter could sustain convincingly. Yet overall there was much in both performance and production to admire: Gareth Lloyd Evans in *Shakespeare Survey 22* particularly commended 'the brilliantly controlled and realized comic scenes', which for him 'underlined the dangerous absurdity of playing with the devil's fire'.

This company returned to the play (or something like it) on

26 August 1974 at Edinburgh's Lyceum Theatre, and then at the Aldwych in London. Here John Barton directed Ian McKellen in a heavily cut version of the text boldly interlaced with extracts from P. F.'s *Damnable Life*. Barton's justification for expunging many of the comic scenes was typically academic: 'Though in theory the sub-plots provide a complementary comment on the main action by showing the abuse of necromantic powers in trivial pranks, in practice they tend to trivialise the tone of the play itself.' However, it might be argued that in cutting much of the ancillary interest the director was evading his responsibilities. Certainly the ambiguity that Coghill and Williams brought to the fore was missing, and such ironic comedy as remained after the cuts went for very little. On the other hand, the use of puppets and masks to suggest the illusory nature of Faustus's satisfactions was highly effective.

Not all recent productions have been elaborate affairs. In the spring of 1970 Gareth Morgan achieved very satisfactory results with a small cast in a basic studio setting for the Royal Shakespeare Company's Theatregoround troupe, in which David Waller was a sturdy Faustus and Alan Howard made a profound impression as Mephostophilis. Even more striking was a not dissimilar presentation, mounted by Christopher Fettes at the Lyric Studio, Hammersmith, on 25 February 1980, with James Aubrey as Faustus, this presentation later switching to the Fortune Theatre. A 'black box' setting contained an all-male cast, and, as in versions directed by Jerzy Grotowski in Poland in 1963 and by Charles Marowitz at the Glasgow Citizens' Theatre in the late sixties, the principal feature was a long refectory table or reading-desk. The late Patrick Magee's Beckettian Mephostophilis was highly praised; some felt it to be the definitive twentieth-century rendition.

This necessarily terse outline may fittingly conclude with a provincial production, of which there have been several since 1980. On 17 September 1981 *Faustus* opened at the Royal Exchange Theatre, Manchester, directed by Adrian Noble, and featuring the then relatively uncelebrated Ben Kingsley, with James Maxwell as Mephostophilis. Since then, Marlowe's tragedy has continued to attract attention, despite its mixed fortunes at the hands of a variety of casts, directors, critics, and spectators.

The following pages place particular emphasis on four presentations which range from the radical to the conservative, the romantic to the anti-heroic, the textually simple to the textually complex. All offer wide differences for analysis; all demonstrate the vitality of a dramatic work whose surface directors have perhaps begun to penetrate only now.

8   Selecting the Text

Possibly the most vital decision a director of *Faustus* takes concerns the script. While considerations of venue, technical resources, and timing are paramount, questions of textual taste and preference also arise. Should either the A-text or the B-text be selected as it stands? Should the most acceptable portions of each be conflated to form a new whole? How relevant are scholarly opinions as to what is and what is not Marlowe's personal handiwork? Does 'directorial interpretation' include abandoning those parts of the play which do not support a particular reading?

Obviously, recourse to a more or less complete text of either the A- or B-version of *Faustus* involves making decisions on the manner in which the hero is to be characterised. The squib-hurling, leg-pulling extrovert of the full texts proves something of an embarrassment to those wishing to cast him as the precursor of Hamlet or Othello. Fewer directors have opted for fidelity to the script as an integrated whole than to their idealised conception of Faustus as the Elizabethan tragic hero and have cut heavily to realise it. The prevailing attitude towards the play's theme must also involve defining the dramatic quality and relevance of the papal- and imperial-court scenes and of the 'low' comedy of Robin, Dick and Horse-Courser. We need to consider how far the choice of text in the productions selected for scrutiny affected the director's interpretation, and conversely how the director's concept of the play and its leading character was reflected in the adaptation made for performance.

Reluctance to accept either the A- or B-text in its entirety can stem from the belief that Marlowe's basic design has been tainted by the corrupting intervention of others, and that the scenes of foolery and knockabout are harmful to the tragic vision and require to be expunged. In 1948 the producer Basil Ashmore published a text featuring 'the removal of non-Marlovian dross' with the aim of disentangling genuine Marlowe from 'degrading interpolations'. The notion that all these passages are not necessarily interpolated, may not 'degrade' the rest of the play, and may well be from Marlowe's brain if not his pen, was slow to be accepted, and is often treated with suspicion even today, as John Barton's remarks quoted earlier make clear. However, the idea has now won currency that it was not a basic aim of the play's designer to portray Faustus as totally admirable.

Before this inhibiting factor was removed, directors must have approached the textual dilemma strongly suspecting that they were about to do less than justice to Marlowe's original vision. William Poel's decision to rely mainly on the 1604 text for his 1896 production was possibly influenced by academic opinion that the 1616 version was a contaminated rendering of its predecessor, but by cutting or playing down episodes which revealed the more frivolous, less reputable side of Faustus, Poel was able to sustain his view that Marlowe intended his protagonist to be 'a titanic character' waging war on the gods. Furthermore, as a result of interpolating tableaux at those Chorus lines which describe how Faustus learnt 'the secrets of astronomy' and later went to 'prove cosmography' [Chorus 1, 2, 20], Poel sustained his focus on the scholar avid for new knowledge, an aspect (in Nicholas Brooke's view) central to a balanced assessment of what Faustus actually achieves through the pact. For the same reason, much of the farcical slapstick was omitted and potentially demeaning scenes given such solemnity as befitted Poel's concept of tragedy. As Allan Wade discovered in 1925, it is impossible to sustain an overall impression of Faustus's innate dignity of character or heroic sense of purpose if his larks with the Horse-Courser and Benvolio are retained. Orson Welles's revival at New York in

1937 further demonstrated the wisdom of tactfully removing anything which might sully Faustus's reputation for serious-ness as well as prevent the performance from being completed in ninety minutes.

Walter Hudd in 1946 appears to have been the first to pioneer the use of the B-text with a minimum of cuts, bravely including the Horse-Courser episode, the tavern scene and the extension of Scene xvii by the irruption of the yokels into the Duke of Vanholt's court. One must admire his unwillingness to falsify the text, but as a result he encountered difficulties similar to those experienced by Wade in 1925. Robert Harris, attempt-ing a romantic rendition of the character, had problems maintaining an air of rarefied scholarship amidst exhibitions of conjuring and horseplay in which he was the leading partici-pant.

William Poel's decision to dovetail the A and B texts to form a new whole was followed by Clifford Williams in 1968, who also showed a bias towards the simpler A version. The clowns, the Horse-Courser, the Knight at Charles V's court all appeared, but the A-text's relegation of farce and spectacle to a less dominant role in the total structure may have helped to ease Eric Porter's search for coherence and consistency in Marlowe's hero. Because he did not idealise Faustus or minimise his complexity, Williams perhaps achieved the greatest recent success in conveying the essentially paradoxical nature of the hero's personality. As a result his Faustus may have had difficulty in fusing the diverse facets into one credible amalgam without making the figure appear a mass of inconsis-tencies, but at least the ambivalence of one's response to him was not evaded.

Michael Benthall's 1961 production involved a more eclectic use of texts; like Poel before him, he excised a number of comedy sequences, all tending to accentuate Faustus's fond-ness for trickery and practical jokes: the Horse-Courser disappeared, along with the tavern scene and the yokels' intrusion at the Vanholt court; Faustus and Mephostophilis no longer rescued Bruno from the papal clutches. The cutting of Faustus's queries concerning Hell in Scene v helped to make him seem less arrogantly cocksure as to the impossibility of his own damnation, and the omission of the discussion on astronomy with Mephostophilis in Scene vi saved him from loss of face in having to admit that 'these slender questions Wagner can decide'. One sensible decision was to delay Faustus's confession of his inability to repent [vi] until nearer the end of the play, just prior to the visit to Rome, which the director placed *after* the episodes at the court of the Emperor. The Knight still received his horns, but only the grape incident remained from the scene with the Vanholts. Faustus's serious feats here assumed greater prominence, and, since the foolery of Robin was completely missing, Wagner taking over some but not all of his functions, this, together with the loss of the devils Banio and Belcher, the Vintner and the goblet, the Carter and the Hostess, ensured that what comedy remained was outweighed by the general air of gravity. It certainly increased the impact of such incidents as the Pope's banquet, which the youthful high spirits of Paul Daneman's Faustus made more acceptable and yet more unseemly.

Benthall's elimination or modification of much of the comedy threw the serious aspects of the drama into relief. In much the same way Fettes in 1980 felt justified in suppressing all the knockabout humour arising from the encounter between Faustus and Benvolio at Charles V's court, as well as the Vanholt scene in its entirety. The Horse-Courser suffered his customary removal, and the tavern scene was also eradicated. Wagner, Robin and Dick were confined to the early part of the action, Fettes employing the A-version of their scenes; this had the effect of concentrating any laughter arising from their amateur conjuring-acts to one area rather than spreading it through the action as a whole. The supply of comedy suddenly dried up. Moreover, with the loss of Benvolio the central focus of the court scenes became the masque of Alexander, swiftly followed by the apparition of Helen, all the contrasting activities which intervene in the texts having gone. This gave a degree of monotony to Faustus's achievements, and a single dimension to his medley of warring aspirations, producing an unbalanced response to him. Yet, not unreasonably, the astronomical discussion was curtailed and the discovery of Faustus's body by the Scholars was not allowed to compromise the grand finale of his 'hellish fall'.

The most radical approach to the text was John Barton's in

1974. He too cut out much of the so-called subplot, his reasons appearing to be those of a fastidious scholar reverting to the conclusion that such scenes trivialised the tone and were dispensable. Again Robin, Dick and their escapades went out, though the Horse-Courser survived; more surprisingly, out went the scenes at the Vatican in their entirety, possibly because Barton chose to set the entire action in Faustus's study. However, he did not hesitate to fill in the resultant gaps with material of his own devising, including a seemingly pointless semi-bawdy episode of erotic intrigue and sexual innuendo between the pregnant Duchess of Vanholt and Faustus, which not only unnecessarily emphasised the scholar's lasciviousness but detracted somewhat from the entranced rhapsody to Helen following hard on its heels. Barton's other major interpolations came from the *Damnable Life*, large portions of which helped to supply the audience with a framework of comment, the narrative being delivered principally by the devils, who also spoke most of the choruses, including the last. The use of such a running commentary did enable spectators more easily to resist becoming unduly involved with Faustus himself, and to remain detachedly observing 'the form of Faustus' fortunes', but it also gave the impression that the diabolic narrators were controlling the action. Many interpolated touches were notable, the most telling being Mephostophilis's response to Faustus's request for advice:

> Were I a man as thou
> And God had once adorn'd me with thy gifts
> Then whiles God breath'd within me would I strive
> By humbling of myself and holy prayers,
> To win eternal joy within his Kingdom.

These lines taken almost verbatim from P. F.'s book gave the impression in the theatre that the demon was certain enough of Faustus's despair to know his sound advice would prove futile, but generally the additions from the *Damnable Life* tended to make one feel that one's response was being monitored. Not enough was left to the spectator's own judgement.

Faustus is clearly a play which invites directorial interference. Neither of its texts is sufficiently authoritative ever to be regarded as sacrosanct, and few producers seem prepared to

take the play as it stands on trust. Most seem content to retain
the scenes covering Faustus's initial decision and those devoted
to his last days, but almost everything in between has been
subjected to modification and excision: the clowning of Robin
and Dick, the unfortunate Horse-Courser, the tavern scene, the
intrusion at the Vanholts' have all suffered. The elimination
of such material can produce an unbalanced effect, a loss of
pleasing variety, as well as reducing the psychological interest
of Faustus himself. In several cases, not even the papal
sequences or the scenes set at the Emperor's court, especially
those in which Benvolio (or in the A-text the Knight) features,
have been excluded from excision, leaving something of a
vacuum at the play's centre. The scene in which Faustus's body
is discovered is another favourite candidate for removal. This
last is a minor matter, but in general terms one might wish that
a few more directors would present the tragedy in a manner as
close as possible to the way it was first written, and permit it to
be judged in that form.

9   PLAYING THE PARTS

For the actor of Faustus, the basic problem obviously lies in
reconciling the varying aspects of the character's complex
nature: is his love of horseplay and practical joking a basic facet
of his personality, or something which only manifests itself once
the bargain with Lucifer is struck? Should the player convey the
impression of a noble mind o'erthrown, or of a man in whom
noble aspiration and petty desires have been inextricably
mixed from the start? Much will depend on the text selected: as
we have seen, Poel, Welles, Benthall and others simplified the
complexities by eliminating or toning down scenes in which
Faustus appears as a mere flashy conjuror or showman for
whom the main asset obtained from his contract seems to be the
right to fool and bamboozle others with impunity. Yet the
complete text can be treated as providing us with a much more
interesting if paradoxical case-history, of a man whose loftier
intellectual ambitions are compromised by a fatal tendency to

cut a dash, to bask in applause, to make fun of the less gifted, to indulge in his own need for sensual gratification. Directors and actors have too rarely sought to assimilate Faustus's contradictory impulses.

William Poel in 1896 encouraged D. L. Mannering to present the Doctor as a serious-minded student anxious for knowledge, a sober interpretation which Shaw praised as being executed 'conscientiously, punctually, and well' (*Saturday Review*, 11 July 1896), even if he found the presentation in general lacking in 'all impetuosity and spontaneity of execution'. Mannering was in fact only seventeen, a virtual newcomer to the stage when he acted for Poel, and this may have accentuated the deliberation with which he played Faustus. Certainly, the *Daily Telegraph* for 3 July judged him to be 'at times a little too quiet and undemonstrative'. His successor, Hubert Carter, a man of 'taurine physique with a strong flexible voice' (Robert Speaight), was less well liked in the revival of 1904, J. T. Grein in the *Sunday Times* for 30 October finding his an uneven performance, with voice and emotional powers not always under control. But one senses that this may not always work to a Faustus's detriment; Grein admitted that Carter presented the sixteenth-century scholar as 'a modern man swayed by feelings to which he gave a wholly unstilted expression', so that he may have contributed that element of emotional dynamism missing from Mannering's more stately and restrained performance.

The question of Faustus's implied age may occupy us for a moment. Several notable players of the role have been relatively young men – Mannering was seventeen, Welles twenty-two, James Aubrey thirty two – and Welles and Aubrey were both able to bring to the part a vigour and enthusiasm which enhanced the fervour of Faustus's ambitions yet rendered his high scholarly reputation less easy to credit, Renaissance precocity notwithstanding. However, the more usual age for the player of Faustus has been between roughly thirty-five and forty – Ion Swinley at thirty-four, Daneman and McKellen at thirty-five, Kingsley at thirty-seven, Burton and Eric Porter at forty. These players could more successfully convey the impression that Faustus had only become dissatisfied with his human limitations after some years spent building a distinguished career, thereby having some justification for finally straying into dangerous territory. Yet the actor cannot afford to be much older than forty: Faustus must after all in literal terms have a life-expectancy of twenty-four years ahead of him when the bargain is struck, and yet it must look sufficiently plausible that he should demand Helen as his mistress towards the end of that term! Robert Harris, forty-six when he ventured on the part, was by no means too old to put across the ardour of the lines to Helen, but conveyed that it was the *idea* of Helen of Troy rather than her physicality that was desired. It is hard to see how Cedric Hardwicke, fifty-five when he took the role in 1948, could ever have been totally successful. Ivor Brown rather severely suggested that, whereas Marlowe's hero is shown as 'pulsing with repressed vitality', Sir Cedric never struck him 'as pulsing with anything' (*Observer*, 10 October 1948), while Peter Fleming in the *Spectator* for 15 October found that 'this Faustus is as much a stranger to passion as to poetry': the apostrophe to Helen lacked the right note of tremulous worship. Perhaps the soundest approach is to cast an actor who can suggest a balanced blend of youth 'hot for certainty' and a mature disenchantment with success that does not arise merely from adolescent petulance or a passing phase of fashionable cynicism.

At the same time, the wrong kind of maturity carries with it the temptation to make of Faustus too dignified and honourable a figure, a tendency which has already been observed to be at odds with large portions of the text. Ion Swinley, a 'fine romantic actor' (James Agate), with a voice J. C. Trewin has remembered as 'deep, true, unmarred by theatrical *vibrato*', discovered this in 1925 when many found his upright, grave, selfless don incongruously ill at ease amid the savage humour and ignoble strife of the central scenes. Elsewhere there was much to praise in Swinley's 'fine response to the exaltation of the Doctor's soaring mind and to the far-flung sweep of his ambition' (Ivor Brown, *Saturday Review*, 31 October 1925), but the impression lingered during the middle episodes that the actor 'had lost interest in the journey and was pursuing it only in expectation of the concluding rewards' (*The Times*, 27 October). A similar feeling arose in connection with Robert Harris's interpretation of 1946–7. Harris, whose 'grave nobility' was his dominant feature, excelled at those places where one might expect tragic passion to command the stage: J. C. Trewin wrote that 'He lets the call to Helen caress the air, and – set against the sky's empty arch – he conveys much of the man's utterable loneliness and last anguish. . .' (*Observer*, 14 July 1946).

But again the inclusion of much of the middle part of the action did not accord with Harris's portrayal; *The Times* for 11 April 1947 was inclined to blame Walter Hudd for giving the actor 'no chance to suggest a powerful mind indulging a sardonic and rather terrifying humour' which forced Harris 'to concentrate on what is kindly and pathetic in the rash scholar'. The director's defenders might have argued that the player's own personality precluded any other emphasis. For the type of performance the *Times* critic hoped for, it would be necessary to wait for Eric Porter.

If Harris's Faustus was too ascetic and remote for many tastes, Paul Daneman in 1961 could be faulted for being too engaging and clubbable. Although he won the audience's sympathy and spoke the lines with conviction, too little was made of the man's fatal flaws of personality, so that his damnation became vaguely unreasonable instead of partially justified. *Punch* found this Faustus 'an attractive and convivial fellow who has outstripped his colleagues in learning and whose only weakness is a fatal ambition to be really famous' (30 August), though even this aspiration did not seem to be the all-consuming obsession it must appear if the magnitude of Faustus's act is to be truly understood. Daneman became too much one of ourselves, a cheery and amicable extrovert eager for success, but who largely failed to convey the hypnotic effect or the quasi-divine status of a magic which could 'ravish' a man of a questing Renaissance temperament. Philip Hope-Wallace in the *Guardian* for 23 August offered the most balanced critical assessment:

Paul Daneman, who is a likeable actor, began in much too cavalier a manner; the entry into this dark world of ghostly temptation and deep doubt needs to be more subtle and awed. He dashed his books aside like a naughty schoolboy . . . from being a rough laughing cavalier he went on in the magic scenes to no higher status than that of a conjuror in a Sinbad outfit. But he redeemed all this with the

genuine passion which he brought to the great scene of Faustus's
last hour. Convulsed and clawing at salvation, he let none of the
mighty lines escape their full significance and the tension mounted
right to the climax without falling away. . . .

If Daneman made Faustus too sympathetic by stressing his
normality and high spirits, Richard Burton in Nevill Coghill's
1966 production was guilty of overemphasising a neurotic
vulnerability. Deliberately eschewing the anticipated romantic
interpretation, Burton portrayed the Doctor as an unprepos-
sessing, rather pathetic pedant employing diabolic powers to
obtain satisfactions his physical inadequacies and chosen
vocation denied him: Irving Wardle recalled 'a bandy-legged
little scholar seizing on magic to act out his frustrated sexual
fantasies' (*The Times*, 28 June 1968). This presentation of a
'sedentary, bespectacled, provincial dominie, celebrating a
windfall of premium bonds with a jaunt round the tourist traps
of Elizabethan Europe' (*Sunday Telegraph*, 20 February 1966),
though an enterprising reading, not only reduced Faustus's
stature and ruled out any laudable aspect to his ambitions, but
also introduced a false incongruity into the play, with exalted
sentiments and thrilling language emanating from a totally
unheroic figure. The encounter with Helen of Troy became
ridiculous, and the final shattering soliloquy lacked the full
sense of human waste. This branch never could have grown full
straight.

It seems essential that a successful Faustus should retain
something of his pristine Renaissance promise even in an age
which places the accent on his human fallibility and folly. Yet
if, in seeking for nobility and grandeur, the player distances
himself too far from us, we lose interest, or find him awkwardly
unconvincing in those parts of the action which show him
stooping to acts of pettiness or feats of showmanship. Yet to
place the accent on the impressario is equally misleading: the
showman was too prominent, for instance, in Vernon Dobtcheff's 1957 portrayal for the OUDS, when throughout the play
the figure smacked too much of the 'accomplished mountebank' (*The Times*, 6 March 1957). Dobtcheff's task was not a
simple one for a student actor: Coghill as director sought to
present a scholar releasing latent desires no longer in need of

suppression, so that his academic aspirations seemed compatible with a taste for riches, power, love, farcical horseplay or sensual sensation. However, it is not easy to contain these within a single *persona* even if 'Faustus must embrace all experience with equal relish and be as vigorous in farce as he is grave in debate and tormented in tragedy' (John Cox, 'On a Production of *Dr Faustus* (1957)' in J. Lawlor and W. H. Auden (eds), *To Nevill Coghill from Friends*, 1966). Dobtcheff's portrait at least recognised the plurality of Faustus's traits, and sought to reconcile them, but the wizard–magus predominated.

In the same way Eric Porter was called on in 1968 to impose a unifying stamp on a complex character full of seeming contradictions. The keynote of his rendering seemed to be an embittered and weary sense of futility, coupled with a sardonic sense of humour, which worked best in the central scenes where the hero amuses himself cynically at the expense of others. What was missing in the earlier scenes was something of that ardent enthusiasm for life and achievement that those essaying a less ambiguous presentation had achieved. Eric Shorter in the *Daily Telegraph* voiced this reservation in his review of 28 June:

> We need to share and be swept up by the magic and the mystery and the passion of the Doctor's desire to conquer the secret forces of nature. And Eric Porter, despite his bold and always intelligent acting, cannot command that power. He himself seems too full of doubts . . . his final speech before the Devil claims him displays a glimpse of that demonic possession which should inform and inflame the play from start to finish. . . .

Other critics found a disconcerting lack of motivation in Porter's performance. Mary Holland in *Queen* (7 July) felt that 'no thought seems to have been given to the character of Faustus, no attempts made to show why he sold his soul'; Irving Wardle in *The Times* for 28 June claimed that the player took things as they came 'without supplying any connecting thread or suggesting what drove a man of godlike intellect to shut his mind to the prospect of damnation. Certainly there are several Fausts: the magician, the clown, the scientist – but it is up to the actor to choose between them. . . .' Yet it could be argued that some actors may think it more important to suggest *all* the facets of the character, and Gareth Lloyd Evans in the *Guardian* for 28 June, who found Porter preserving the line of the character and adding to it 'his own beautifully spoken marble-fronted passion', and J. C. Trewin in the *Illustrated London News* for 6 July were more impressed. For the latter, the actor was

> the most impressive Faustus I have known in the theatre. . . . Eric Porter has real authority. At first eagerly and arrogantly resolved, he can suggest the range of the man's questing mind. We understand Faustus's intellectual pride. . . . When it is time to scale the crest he is there, invoking the spirit of Helen with a controlled passion that keeps the speech from being an actor's showpiece, and then using his powerful imagination in the desolate horror of the close. . . .

Yet it is significant that Trewin found less to commend in the central sequences, where one felt that this austerely ironic Faustus would have realised the triviality of his meretricious exploits and desisted. At times Faustus seemed too detached from what was happening. Neither face to face with Helen nor confronted with his own impending demise did the excitement of the sexual encounter or the horror of annihilation really communicate itself. While lacking Harris's lofty romantic air, Porter also seemed a little too remote from human concerns.

A different kind of detachment informed Ian McKellen's performance in 1974 for John Barton. Confined within his study, this Faustus was a closet fantasist, an interpretation supported by the fact that none of the magical phenomena was presented as substantial, taking the form of dummies, puppets, masked creations, and dolls intended to beguile the bemused scholar into believing in the actuality of 'palpable trash'. This certainly reinforced the notion that Hell is a state of mind, but it forced McKellen to express much of the external action in terms of his own darting, twitching, writhing body. Milton Shulman in the *Evening Standard* for 6 September took the production to task for this:

> This is a very busy performance with hardly a moment when the good doctor isn't leaping about for a precious book, nudging the servants of Lucifer for some reaction to his activities, gleefully hugging himself at his own cleverness, or thrashing about in fearful agony as he prepares to meet his doom. A little more repose might make a more convincing philosophical Faustus.

Yet, for all his contorted hyperactivity, McKellen remained essentially a man moving and hallucinating as if in a drugged sleep, 'a sad, haunted sinner in a light tenor voice' (John Barber). Some reviewers liked this 'enchanted slothfulness', but others, like Garry O'Connor in *Plays and Players* for October 1974, found it 'full of tormented mannerism', although this critic thought that John Barton had saddled the performer with an impossible task by directing so much attention onto him. As with Burton, too, too heavy a stress was given to Faustus's neurotic individuality, too little placed on those defects of character shared with us all. As John Barber trenchantly expressed it in the *Daily Telegraph* for 9 September,

> By censoring the Vatican scenes [the production] denies his zest and impertinence. . . . By turning the Good and Bad Angels into glove-puppets worked by Faustus, it makes him a schizophrenic invalid, not a rebel thinker shackled by a hostile moral order. By making the vision of Helen a paltry marionette, it sterilises the ineluctable lure of flesh-and-blood sensuality. In short, it makes Faustus a deluded nut . . . and not a magnificent over-reacher doomed to the fate of Icarus.

Against this should be set some remarks of Michael Billington in the *Guardian* for 6 September:

> the strength of Ian McKellen's performance is that it supplies an internal dialectic only thinly expressed in the text. On the one hand, he is a bushy-haired peasant scholar whose arching catlike body is full of yearning lusts; on the other hand, he is a tormented over-reacher suddenly prey to fits of rational sadness. And McKellen's own peculiar acting style, in which his frame seems to be possessed by some emotional Dybbuk, admirably fits the concept of a Faustus who has become a battleground for penitence and despair.

But it might still be urged that there is more to Faustus and his wishes than delusion and fantasy, and that an actor must seek to bring out the positive as well as the negative aspects of his aspiration. In this, McKellen's somewhat mannered vocal delivery, nasal and often high-pitched, was an undoubted handicap.

In this respect the relative youthfulness of James Aubrey's playing in 1980 was an asset: the zest and bounce many critics missed in Ian McKellen was certainly found in Aubrey's adolescent-seeming hero. Yet the result was that the accent now fell on the pangs of a frustrated student rather than those of a mature professor; the focus shifted from Faustus's intellectual appetites to his sexual desires, which while present in the original tended to become overstressed in a production where, with an all-male cast, sensual needs perforce took on homosexual colouring. Like Daneman James Aubrey was an essentially likable actor, and his boyish energy was infectious, but, in addition to finding his vocal range limited, several critics missed a sense of intellectual weight and experience. Thomas Turgeon wrote in the *Theatre Journal*, vol. 32 (1980), that the most striking feature of Aubrey's performance was its naïveté. 'Here there is no great scholar who has exhausted the limits of man's knowledge. Rather, he seems to be an impatient young man who's sick of school.' Others spoke of 'an academic whizzkid', and 'a Wittenberg *Wunderkind*', and, while there was praise for Aubrey's ability to suggest moral weakness, mental shallowness and physical dynamism, the general view was that Faustus's initial potential for achievement and his noble defiance when confronting Mephostophilis were not sufficiently brought out. He remained a difficult postgraduate appealing for help with his thesis.

A charge of excessive youthfulness could scarcely be levelled at Ben Kingsley's slight, balding Faustus at Manchester in 1981; aiming like Burton at an unheroic portrayal, this actor was at his happiest in the scenes of irreverence and trickery, less so at suggesting a coherent interpretation of the character which would embrace all his wide-ranging moods. Irving Wardle in *The Times* for 18 September felt that Kingsley gave 'no clear sign of precisely who Faustus is or what he most wants. He touches on intellectual pride, sensuality, and the spirit of Renaissance inquiry. But as he leaves all these open, there is no centre to the character.' John Barber in the *Daily Telegraph* on the following day felt that, while Kingsley could suggest 'the darkly troubled soul of a man never wholly committed either to God or devil', he failed 'in his eloquent rapture over un-Godly things. Here the actor's lack of presence and his dry nasal intonation betray his difficulty with a heroic role.' Once again, reservations were expressed about a performance that had much to commend it. A totally satisfying rendition of the part of Faustus continues to elude even our most enterprising actors.

This is far less true of those playing Mephostophilis. In many productions the performance of the demon has often been deemed to outshine that of the protagonist, the main reason being that a consistent portrait is more easily achieved. Actors do not have to contend with an apparent change of personality in the middle portion of the play, as many claim they have to with Faustus, the demon's role here being largely to egg the doctor on. The part is economical and effective, and as such is not an exacting one for the right player.

Mephostophilis contrasts with the energetic, scurrying, mischievous devils of medieval stage tradition: his solemn dignity and melancholy weariness of spirit offer a visible indication of the pangs of godless existence. It is also his function to pretend to support Faustus in his activities, retaining a courteous bearing which disarms and flatters his victim, only manifesting his viciousness when Faustus looks like recanting. Any suggestion of psychological complexity stems from his ambiguous position in hinting to Faustus of perils he knows the scholar is too infatuated with magic to shy away from: he is himself in Hell, a Hell which his prey deems a fable.

Early interpretations of the part appear to have erred towards a simplistic if efficient keynote: Shaw found Dennis Eadie, who played the part for Poel in 1896, 'as joyless and leaden as a devil need be', though in 1904 the *Daily Telegraph* expressed its displeasure at the 'slow, woebegone, sepulchral delivery' of Eadie's successor, George Ingleton, and C. E. Montague disliked his 'unbroken gloom'. The temptation to exaggerate or romanticise the role is always there: in the *Observer* for 1 November 1925 St John Ervine dismissed Ernest Thesiger's portrayal as 'conceived by Aubrey Beardsley rather than by Marlowe', though *The Times* for 27 October commended his 'curious mingling of spite and dignity' and James Agate praised him for a 'flawless' invocation 'of a spirit fallen from nobleness, and of a hell whose fiends are filled not with delight but weariness'. It was this 'full dark weariness' that J. C. Trewin missed in Hugh Griffith's performance at Stratford in 1946, though he approved of his avoidance of 'brimstone-melodrama'. Two years later Robert Eddison at the Old Vic essayed a stance loftier and more aloof that Griffith's; his 'gaunt, nervous friar' with 'the look and sound of a damned soul' (*Guardian*, 9 October 1948) avoided any suggestion of the comradely note which was a feature of one or two subsequent renditions, culminating in Patrick Magee's memorable creation in 1980. The *Spectator* (15 October) also missed in Eddison 'those flashes of gleeful malevolence which one expects'.

More recent productions have brought out more of the complexity of Mephostophilis, to such an extent that a number of critics have discovered the core of interest in the helpless foreknowledge of the demon rather than the human folly of Faustus. The suave flatterer was uppermost in Michael Goodliffe's performance in 1961; here one had the courteous but determined fiend in the Thesiger tradition, cloaking 'with a humorous eye his steely determination to get what he wants' (*Punch*, 30 August). However, there was nothing truly fearful about Goodliffe's depiction of damnation, even when he threatened torments, and Trewin felt that he failed to convey 'the terrible loneliness of the spirit'. The demon remained well mannered and civilised to the last. Seven years later Terrence Hardiman presented a subtler figure, fairly summarised by Gareth Lloyd Evans in *Shakespeare Survey 22* (1969):

> The pathos of this play comes from our observation of a man wasting great gifts and entering into a trap. It was Terrence Hardiman's Mephostophiles [*sic*], rather than Faustus, who induced the pity of it in a performance characterized by quiet grief, mordant humour, and resigned dignity.

Furthermore Hardiman and Porter achieved a moving sense of *rapport* as Faustus stumbled towards the true nature of his bargain, effectively achieved at the end when 'Mephostophilis, now viciously demonic, yet laid a hand on Faustus' head in an almost tender farewell, while the latter uttered his final "ah *Mephastophilis*" as an agonized cry for help' (Verna Ann Foster, '*Dr Faustus* on the Stage').

This bond was less in evidence between Ian McKellen and Emrys James in 1974 partly because McKellen's Faustus was conceived as making meaningful contact with no one. As a result James spent much of the play standing by, coldly watching his mesmerised prey and wearing 'the cold sad smile of one who knows immeasurably more than his mundane master will ever think to ask' (Jeremy Kingston, *Punch*, 18 September). 'Cool, ironical and unblinking' (*Guardian*), this Mephostophilis was clearly in control, manipulating his deluded prize without a flicker of sympathy or fellow-feeling for one to join him shortly in the ranks of the damned.

But pride of place must undoubtedly be accorded to Patrick Magee's masterly and memorable portrayal for Christopher Fettes in 1980. Here was a Mephostophilis for the late twentieth century, sharing clear affinities with some of Magee's definitive appearances in Samuel Beckett roles. As Michael Scott writes in *Renaissance Drama and a Modern Audience*,

> Magee's presence influenced the complete production. His doleful sunken eyes within his dachshund face, his fatigued step and his chilling intoned voice with its heavy stress on final syllables, produced the resignation of evil. Faustus's enthusiasm was an absurdity confronted with this sadly-deep old man.

Such a Mephostophilis conveyed more eloquently than any of his predecessors the eternal pains which awaited Faustus and made his scholar's arrogance the more tragic, but it had the disturbing effect of transferring one's sympathies from the errant moral to the damned spirit. Of the bond created between hunter and hunted Irving Wardle wrote well in *The Times* for 28 March 1980:

> His relationship with Faustus is an extraordinary blend of honesty and trickery. Never removing his burning eyes from his prey, he chaperones Faustus like an indulgent old tutor, and something indistinguishable from affection grows up between them, with Faustus even nuzzling into his shoulder like a child.

The effect of Magee's extraordinarily gripping performance was to turn the play inside out, and yet demonstrate the theatrical riches which still lie embedded in the text awaiting release. Mephostophilis became a passive and helpless spectator of Faustus's ruin, an almost fatherly figure hopelessly watching his son slide down the slippery slope as he had once slid himself. Here was a mournful pitying creature able to sympathise with

those who dare the unknown and risk inevitable disappointment, since he too had aspired and fallen in his turn. Devil and
damned thus shared a common experience of the fate of God's
inevitably disobedient creatures. It is an approach to the play
which may yet be developed further.

10   SETTING THE STAGE

One of the major problems for any director of *Faustus* has been
to unite its disparate elements into a satisfying whole, and in
this quest the mode of staging chosen is central. William Poel in
1896, by insisting on conditions approximating to those of an
Elizabethan playhouse, concentrated the action using a
method others have sought to emulate since. These directors
have felt impelled to follow suit partly because of the lack of
public familiarity with Marlowe compared with Shakespeare,
which has persuaded them to ensure intimacy and immediacy
at all costs. The danger then is that Marlowe's plays come to be
seen as no more than collector's pieces; yet their revival has
certainly benefited from a recognition of what open platforms
and thrust stages have to offer.

The *Morning Post* of 3 July 1896 provides a detailed descrip-
tion of Poel's flexible stage-setting and its unifying effect on
Faustus:

> The front curtain open reveals a room of which the back is in two
> storeys, each with its own curtain. . . . The farcical and other
> interludes . . . took place in front of the stage with the principal
> curtains closed. When Lucifer appeared, it was on the balcony
> behind, the apparition being rendered more demoniacal by the
> addition of one or two attendant devils and by red fire and smoke.
> The lower curtains at the back when opened revealed a great
> dragon's mouth wide open, representing the mouth of hell. Out of
> this came Mephostopheles [*sic*], and under his escourt the Seven
> Deadly Sins, Alexander and his paramour, and Helen. . . .

As a challenge to the overloaded, heavily scenic, long-winded
Shakespearean revivals of his day, Poel's productions were
revolutionary in their simplicity, and Shaw praised them for

their replacement of 'attempts at an impossible scenic veri-similitude' with 'a few well-understood conventions adroitly handled' (*Saturday Review*, 11 July 1896). Yet their multiple curtained cavities sound clumsy contrasted with Allan Wade's preference for an open, uncluttered stage of his Phoenix Society presentation, even if he sanctioned the inclusion in Norman Wilkinson's permanent setting of an 'inner stage' and balcony on Poel's model. However, Wade 'seemed at his happiest as a producer with a bare stage which gave him complete freedom to design bold movement and strikingly pictorial groupings' (Norman Marshall, *The Other Theatre*, 1947). Reviews of *Faustus* confirm this, James Agate noting that the 1925 performance was as effective as it could be on a purely formalised stage, though evidently the directorial style displayed a Poel-like restraint not to all tastes. 'Severity is the Phoenix note', wrote Agate; St John Ervine dismissed it all as 'spiritless'!

Unremarkably, in view of his venue, Nugent Monck's Canterbury presentation of 1929 employed an open platform backed by an 'inner stage' like Wade's. More surprisingly, Orson Welles and John Houseman made use of a projecting stage in 1937 at the Maxine Elliott Theatre, where, despite Welles's use of modern technical aids, Marlowe's 'Elizabethan-ness' was taken advantage of to bring the play closer to spectators, even those seated in a conventional theatre. The *New York Herald Tribune* for 9 January described the impression received:

> The action takes place against a black background and the players are brilliantly spotlighted against it ... isolated from their surroundings and appearing for most of the time on a stage apron that extends far beyond the proscenium, the effectively costumed actors appear in eerie space. There are trapdoors galore, a handsome series of smoke screens, many shrewd electrical contraptions and all the devices of modern stage art, but the final effect is of a true and simple translation of the Elizabethan stage into contemporary theatrical terms.

To re-create in the modern theatre the impact of the original presentations has been the aspiration of most modern directors, and contemporary experimentation with stage-shapes and auditoria has assisted a return to some of the direct impact and

intimacy enjoyed by the Elizabethans, while imposing a unity
on the play's ingredients. Reviewing Poel's revived production
at the Free Trade Hall, Manchester, in 1904, C. E. Montague
commented on the advantages of the platform stage over 'our
modern picture stage, where the actor is seen in the flat, framed
in a recess, and planted on a background'. To obtain the proper
contrast, however, he argued that 'we spectators would have
had to be sitting on three sides of the stage, which should have
jutted out to just the middle of the pit'. In 1961 at the Assembly
Hall, Edinburgh, Michael Benthall was able to achieve more or
less this effect, assisting audiences to participate in the
spectacle rather than merely to lose themselves in an illusion.
By appearing on a brightly lit platform with spectators to three
sides of them and by using the gangways of the hall for exits and
entries, the players made immediate contact with their patrons,
while the director allowed his telling visual effects to impinge
on the auditorium itself, notably with 'the eruption of the
Emperor's court and the Pope's guests on to the dark platform
stage which suddenly [sprang] into blazing colour' (Philip
Hope-Wallace, *Guardian*, 23 August). Benthall's accent on
'multiple comings and goings' (*Punch*) was able to invest the
play with the trappings of a 'brilliant pageant' (*Tatler*) whose
excitements the *Sunday Telegraph* for 17 September vividly
conveyed: 'smoke, sulphur and incense swirled about one;
Pride, in pearly high-buttoned boots, brushed past perfumed.
Silks and satins swished down the aisles. . . .'

However, not everyone was satisfied with the Assembly Hall
arrangement, Hope-Wallace once more supplying an objective
diagnosis:

> there are many places from which the impact of the play . . . is
> diminished or largely dissipated. Mr Benthall uses the built-up
> back of the stage to good purpose, with the angels of good and evil
> standing like winged sentries; and in his great solo scenes Faustus
> does for the greater part manage to share the projection of his
> performance with a wide arc of onlookers.
>
> But for those sitting sideways other scenes are lost; for me at
> least, the crucial scene of the bond-swearing was something
> glimpsed from the wings of a stage, and badly 'masked' at that. In
> other words we do not enjoy either the advantages of theatre in the
> round, or the steady command of the action which we should get in
> a proscenium arch.   (*Guardian*, 23 August)

Be that as it may, when the production transferred to the Old Vic Theatre many deplored the reduction in tension, the loss of involvement, the attempt to cram a quart of dramatic effects into a pint-pot of stage, the play's retreat from close inspection behind the proscenium arch. Effects specifically designed for a particular and idiosyncratic venue proved incapable of transfer to a conventional playhouse: if spectacle was the aim, then not every theatre would prove right for it; if spectacle was not to be the aim, how was a producer to handle somewhat intractable material? The following decades would supply some answers.

Proscenium-style presentation had not invariably proved disappointing: Walter Hudd's Stratford production of 1946–7 won praise for the most elaborately designed scenery erected for the play up to that date. Riette Sturge Moore's permanent set in the neo-Gothic style then fashionable contained several levels linked by tumbling staircases, with a symmetrically balanced pattern of ivied archways silhouetted against a skycloth at the rear. Nevill Coghill too, in 1957, availed himself throughout of a triptych of arches, the central one topped by a cross, although as if to emphasise the director's view of the play as an ambiguous morality drama, the hallowed arches more often than not contained onlookers from the diabolic hierarchy. Like Benthall four years later, Coghill set his angels high on either side of the stage, flanking the action, though not permanently in view. Below the level of the cross, which acted as the study, the main stage area served as the base for the comic action while Hell jutted into the auditorium. A huge book lay on the forestage, whose blank pages Faustus ransacked frantically towards the close, seeking for an answer to his quest:

> this produced a thrill of terror starker than all the grimacing devils and looming black shapes of the previous action. The illusion of Academe was destroyed as devilish hands tore upwards through the pages to drag Faustus to Hell.
>
> (John Cox, 'On a Production of *Dr Faustus*, 1957')

A comparably graphic effect occurred in Williams's 1968 venture:

> Faustus finished his final speech grovelling in abject terror on the ground. The clock finished striking. Nothing happened. After a

long moment Faustus raised his head and looked round the totally
empty stage. He started to laugh. As he reached the hysteria of
relief, the back wall of the stage gave way and fell forward in
sections revealing an ominous red glow and a set of spikes like the
dragon's teeth of the Siegfried Line. The denizens of hell emerged
with a kind of slow continuous shuffle until Faustus was sur-
rounded . . . he was then seized and carried shrieking through the
teeth of hell mouth which closed leaving the wall of Faustus's study
again intact.

(Nigel Alexander, 'The Performance of
Christopher Marlowe's *Dr Faustus*')

This formed the climax of a production whose setting by Farrah
for many lacked something in needful claustrophobia. Faustus's study was rather too bare and unlittered for some tastes,
though Gareth Lloyd Evans in *Shakespeare Survey 22* praised the
absence of 'a vast clutter of dusty books, skulls, astrolabes and
olde mappes', a lack for which John Barton more than atoned
in 1974! Similarly the courts of the Emperor and the Duke, and
the Vatican, were somewhat bleakly and austerely suggested in
1968, especially by contrast with Benthall's splendours: 'the
dark Tudor tomb half lit by candles' (*Guardian*, 28 June) was
too cenotaph-like. By contrast, Michael Annals's Gothic set for
the 1974 revival was overstocked with 'a prodigious clutter of
mediaeval junk' (*Daily Telegraph*, 27 August), only possible
because the action was entirely set in Faustus's study. This
certainly proved to be 'a marvellously claustrophobic and
atmospheric design' (*Plays and Players*, October 1974), but it
could seem distracting, so interesting were its contents, which
included a marvellous clock on which a skeleton appeared to
denote the passage of time. The setting, like McKellen's
performance, was introverted and hypnotic, but it offered no
respite or relief from Faustus's tormented neurotic mind, and
did too little justice to his heroic dreams.

Simple economy of visual effect was the keynote of Kandis
Cook's 1980 setting at the Lyric Studio and the Fortune. As at
Edinburgh, the spectators sat on three sides of the platform; the
bare thrust stage was dominated by a long library desk or
refectory table at which the black-gowned scholars studied.
Stools and a couple of benches were the only other furniture on
the black-curtained arena: there was no trace of Gothic clutter.

At the rear of this acting-area hung a semi-transparent white gauze where the apparitions appeared 'like figures in a mirage' (*Guardian*, 29 March) on a simple rostrum. After so many productions which placed the accent on Renaissance reds and golds, on colourful rituals and costumed parades, Fettes's designer's accent on blacks and whites was refreshing and encouraged an increased concentration on those aspects of the work selected for emphasis. To discuss the dominant impression received from all four major productions under review will be the final task of this study.

11 DELIGHTING THE SENSE

The importance Elizabethan playwrights attached to the visual and aural dimension must always be respected in any worthwhile modern revival. *Faustus* abounds in opportunities for impressive sights and sounds, for colourful costuming and inventive stage effects. Yet there is always the danger that the spectacle will take command, that the eye and ear will be sated while the mind or emotions remain unengaged. Too much pageantry is distracting, and, although some commentators claim that this play requires dressing up and setting to music in order to retain any hold on our attention, most would surely argue that the work can stand on its own without undue decoration. Certainly Gareth Morgan's Theatregoround production of 1970 and the Lyric Studio version of 1980 demonstrated that *Faustus* could be highly effective without elaborate embellishment.

Visually Poel set the tone with his blend of medieval dragon's mouth and Victorian red fire, and the diabolic element is still undoubtedly one feature which has attracted directors and designers to the play. Poel's devils resembled those in the popular paintings and engravings of the fifteenth-century German Martin Schongauer, while Mephostophilis on his first entry recalled a demon from the roof of Notre Dame. Such precision was no doubt attendant on Poel's expressed endeavour 'to strengthen by pictorial aid that part of the play

which is least interesting and profitable as dramatic literature',
but his productions do merit C. E. Montague's stricture that
they formed 'a banquet of tit-bits of antiquarian research and
acute conjecture'. However, one shrewd touch which others
might have developed was to give, in the 1904 revival at least,
Faustus's devil wife a beautiful front, but a skeletal appearance
when she turned her back. (Such a treatment could well be
applied to Helen of Troy, but, to the best of the present writer's
knowledge, never has been.)

Part of the problem with *Faustus* is not so much that, as James
Agate observed, it 'is bound up with the belief in the actual
existence of hideous things with tails', but that the devils need
to be made real to us on stage, or they become intolerably
melodramatic, in spite of the presence of Mephostophilis, a
credible-enough demon because not a cliché of one. Thus *The
Times* for 11 April 1947 took exception to Walter Hudd's devils
as being 'less like many evil grotesques than the creatures of
Christmas pantomime'; for much the same reason Mary
Holland in *Queen* for 7 July 1968 dismissed Clifford Williams's
production as 'good pantomime fun . . . when the joking has to
stop there is nothing else'. Yet Williams's demons were not in
the conventional mould; said *Punch* for 19 July 1968, 'These
creatures of hell are sulphurously horrid, red-eyed and hairy as
beasts.' These tentacular fiends were certainly more terrifying
than the elegant Renaissance devils of Benthall's 1961 Edinburgh version, with Eddison's Lucifer 'dressed up to the nines
in a flame-coloured creation from the lush wardrobe of hell'
(*Punch*, 30 August), though some distorted Bosch-like oddities
also crawled around to some effect. Yet Benthall's emphasis on
colour and style was not necessarily a false one: Hell must not
be presented to Faustus as too repulsive, or he will not be
plausibly allured by it. In this, Adrian Noble's instinct to make
Hell seem fun in his Manchester production of 1981 was sound:
his choirboy devils riding bicycles at least offered Faustus some
prospect of entertainment.

Other directors have found other means of treating Faustus
as deluded: both Barton and Fettes gave their devils a measure
of neutrality as mere figments of a diseased imagination.
Barton clothed them as black-robed monks operating the
puppets that the doctor took for reality; Fettes treated the

demons as identical to those apparitions of Helen, Alexander and the others obsessing Faustus all along; though David Rappaport's dwarf Beelzebub (doubled with the part of the Pope) made a distinct figure. While such tendencies to internalise the cosmic struggle for Faustus's soul have the effect of depleting the spectacle, one suspects that in future this will increasingly be regarded as the best approach to the director's dilemma.

Allied with the diabolic dimension is the presentation of the Good and Bad Angels and the Seven Deadly Sins. We have come some way from Poel's angelic figures, 'their draperies sewn into Botticellian folds and tucks' (Shaw), intoning their lines as if they were plainsong, although as recently as 1961 the Old Vic Good Angel chanted its advice! Then both angels stood at the back of the stage like winged sentries, in keeping with Benthall's iconographic pageantry, providing a constant reminder of the tug-of-war between good and evil. More striking and certainly more in keeping with modern sensibilities was John Barton's notion of giving the angels the form of puppets – a white toy figure and a black voodoo doll – which Ian McKellen both manipulated and supplied the voices for, although the overall conception that Faustus was himself the victim of manipulation was undermined by his needful control over the marionettes. In many respects Fettes's decision to have the angelic voices proceed from Faustus's fellow scholars was happier and less awkward.

The presentation of the Seven Deadly Sins has always presented a challenge and a risk, ever since Shaw complained of the *fin de siècle* quality of Poel's female tribe, 'the five worst of them being so attractive that they got rounds of applause on the strength of their appearance alone'. Once again, part of the point is that Faustus expresses himself 'delighted' with them; either their appearance must be sufficiently delightful not to terrify him or Faustus must be shown to be a victim of an illusion. In this respect Nevill Coghill's 1957 creation of a beautiful masque which none the less carried with it a strong note of menace as its members clung 'to a rapt Faustus in coils that threatened to stifle him' (*The Times*, 6 March 1957) was happily conceived. The parade must not be decorative and nothing else: there must be menace and violence below the surface, and Faustus's jocular disregard of this malevolence must be brought out. Eric Porter conveyed his sense of amusement well in 1968, but, once more, Williams's accent on the ghastliness of Lucifer's hellish 'pastime' ignored Faustus's clearsightedness and his likely resistance to diabolic blandishments. Eric Shorter in the *Daily Telegraph* for 28 June pronounced the Deadly Sins 'a Mardi Gras carnival of mere grotesques, most of them interchangeable and wearing skull-masks', and, though Irving Wardle found both masks and 'grotesquely elongated limbs' indicative of 'authentic creatures of the sulphurous pit' (*The Times*, 28 June), there was some sympathy with Mary Holland's distaste for 'a general atmosphere of suppurating sores, bloated stomachs, and crippled limbs horribly askew' (*Queen*, 7 July).

Again, it was Barton and Fettes who approached the difficulty in the most radical ways. Like Orson Welles in 1937, Barton presented the Sins as puppets, but on this occasion as life-size marionettes in the Japanese Bunraku tradition, worked by the virtually unseen devils in their black habits. This helped to give the Sins substance and interest, while making it clear that their attraction was superficial, and that other forces were literally pulling the strings. Something of the nightmare menace of Envy in the 1968 version was lost, with its 'clutching praying-mantis arms ten feet long' (*Punch*, 10 July), but it became credible that the mesmerised Faustus should wish to visit Hell and see more of such 'delights'. As Michael Billington phrased it in the *Guardian* for 6 September 1974, 'Instead of the usual voluptuous floorshow, as if Pieter Brueghel were working the Talk of the Town, we get a series of wispy, trailing Bunraku-like creature that underline the illusory nature of Faustus's pleasure.'

Christopher Fettes's presentation of the Deadly Sins cannot be detached from his general approach to the supernatural phenomena in the play: setting them all behind his white gauze curtain, he endowed their hazy shapes with an ethereal visionary quality which increased their desirability for Faustus at least. Nowhere was this more true than in the controversial but effective presentation of the figure of Helen as a young man in a filmy trouser suit who achieved an extraordinary erotic rapport with Faustus. The same note of sexual display was marked in the Sins, whose appearance resembled, according to *The Times*, 'a creepy Miss World competition, with demons slouching up the runway to auction their obsessions'.

The presentation of Helen has become one of the major points of interest in discussing the staging of the play, and it has often overshadowed more vital ones. Yet one suspects it is the anticipation of Helen's arrival which persuades some spectators to sit through the central scenes! More seriously, her entry is a crucial incident: winning her love represents both Faustus's finest hour and his most disastrous act, and any production must make it clear that both views are possible. Yet few directors have been prepared to hint at the possibility of Helen's demonic nature: her beauty and allure are usually unequivocal. The problem then becomes to ensure that she should not disappoint her admirers: she must be exceptional, and for this reason Clifford Williams presented her totally naked, with an elaborate coiffure and shining torso. This, instead of making her warmly desirable, had the opposite effect of making her untouchable and unattainable. Yet for some this confirmed Lucifer's duplicity: the Devil had ensured that the scholar would never make Helen his own. If she was 'too Dresden-like for Faustus to touch' (*Daily Telegraph*, 28 June 1968), it seemed right in context.

The question of whether or not Faustus and Helen *should* touch was not new: as early as 1896 objections were raised when Faustus only kissed her hand, and she kissed his forehead! Helen's entry then was simple but effective: she walked upstage towards Faustus with her face virtually obscured from the audience, so that her beauty, taken on trust, could be imagined from Faustus's reaction to its presumed quality. Such an approach is in significant contrast to that adopted in the Manchester production of 1981, where a charismatic Helen was lowered from the flies to the waiting scholar in a shower of fine golden dust. Audiences of today are perhaps less prepared to accept suggestion than in 1896: Helen's perfection must be made obvious, if at all possible.

Again John Barton gave us the most daring treatment of this quasi-divine figure. In 1974, in accordance with the general style of the production, Helen was nothing more than a blonde wig, a mask, and a wisp of chiffon carried about by Faustus, lovingly caressed, and finally taken to bed with him. The loss of living, breathing sexuality was great, yet the possible disappointment attendant on discovering Helen to be less perfect than one's image of her was dispelled, while Faustus's own degradation in the search for physical satisfaction could hardly have been more tellingly conveyed. John Barber's complaint that Barton had thereby sterilised 'the ineluctable lure of flesh-and-blood sensuality' seemed somehow beside the point: yet the dummy Helen could not have succeeded in any other context but one in which Faustus himself was portrayed as a pursuer of dark, secretive joys.

Many aspects of the play remain for discussion, in particular the treatment of the papal tribunal and the banquet, and the scenes set at the imperial court. Both provide ample opportunity for colourful spectacle after the claustrophobia of Faustus's study; both offer chances for inventive business and comic relief; both conceal hidden dangers from directors tempted to treat these scenes as pure padding or a welcome escape from the play's serious concerns. But these aspects of the work can perhaps be most effectively handled if we turn to the play's themes and their treatment in the productions under review.

12 STATING THE THEME

When in 1959, in his autobiography *A Life in the Theatre*, Sir Tyrone Guthrie wrote that one of the minor tragedies of the historical development of European culture had been 'the divorce between the theatrical performance and the literary study of drama', he could scarcely have foreseen the present upsurge of interest in the staging of plays among academics. Few scholars or critics would now come to the discussion of dramatic literature without an acute interest in its stage realisation, or in many cases without some practical knowledge of plays in production, albeit at the amateur level. Yet one drawback to this desirable situation is that, whereas scholarly commentators are frequently prone to perceive and bring out ambiguities and paradoxes within a playtext, and to emphasise the multiplicity of available responses to them, the director of a play in the theatre usually feels obliged to take concrete decisions on what to stress and what to play down. With a work such as *Faustus*, over-emphasis on ambivalence, however admirable in academic terms, can leave spectators baffled; on the other hand, over-insistence on a particular reading can lay a producer open to the charge of limiting our response to a full range of meanings.

There can be little doubt, as Verna Ann Foster points out in her stimulating survey '*Dr Faustus* on the Stage', that early presentations divide into those which treat the story as that of an idealised Renaissance hero whose faults, if any, are those of the justified sinner, and those which view the work as an Elizabethan morality play in which the old lesson of the wages of sin being death is inculcated. William Poel, as we have seen, ignored much that was base or trivial in Faustus's character, and cast him as a serious seeker after truth, reinforcing the point by permitting him to be viewed as both astronomer and cosmographer, and thus anticipating Nicholas Brooke's argument that the middle scenes may not depict Faustus in such a harsh light as some orthodox commentators claim. But in order to achieve this impression directors have had to cut heavily into the text to suppress such slapstick incidents as the fooling with the Horse-Courser, or have played up the solemn majesty of such sights as the vision of the Emperor Alexander. Failure to do the former creates too great a dichotomy between romantic scholar and cocksure magician, as in Wade's production in 1925 and Walter Hudd's in 1946; failure to do the latter reinforces what has been the much more general attitude to the play, that Faustus achieves nothing of real lasting worth from his bargain, just as Lucifer intends.

This of course has been an important feature in the argument of those who interpret *Faustus* as a morality piece: by making his immoral pact with the Devil, the Doctor turns his back on legitimate satisfactions, trading them in for a bag of tricks. Nugent Monck's 1929 presentation, by coupling the play with *Everyman*, foreshadowed the critical approach developed by James Smith, Leo Kirschbaum, Sir Walter Greg and others, but to do so a ruthless line had to be taken with the more commendable, less selfish, motives behind Faustus's decision to hand himself over to diabolic agents. To treat the work as an updated morality does less than justice to the challenge *Doctor Faustus* presents to orthodoxy, and to the picture it offers of a living personality rather than a doctrinal statistic.

In this respect Nevill Coghill's attempt to do justice both to the morality framework and to the integrity of the character-portrait it contains was important: seeing the play as a study of the wages of excessive intellectual curiosity, Coghill was able to unify the aspiring scholar with the conjuring showman by suggesting that any abuse of his magic powers sprang from Faustus's vocational frustrations expressing themselves in pranks and showing-off rather than solid achievements. What did not come across in 1957 or 1966 was that Faustus is partly an heroic figure, even if not the dignified titanic rebel of Poel's version. Neither Dobtcheff's sorcerer nor Burton's bookworm quite measured up to the Renaissance dimension.

Michael Benthall came closest in recent times to a reading of the play which suggested in some measure that Faustus received value for his disastrous bargain. The ceremonial pomp and processions of the Edinburgh version not only ensured that the middle of the play was held together by spectacle, but meant that Faustus himself increased his stature as one who had risen from scholarly obscurity to mingle with the highest in the land, albeit in the case of the Pope to mock them. Certainly, amid the impressive trappings of the imperial court, Faustus came across as a conjuror still, but one expert and awe-inspiring enough to be invited to give a command performance. Paul Daneman here created something of the favourable impact some commentators feel Faustus would have achieved on the Elizabethan stage: the splendid surroundings certainly diminished the sense of his having sacrificed his soul for a few parlour tricks, at least at Edinburgh. At the Old Vic the inevitable reduction in pageantry renewed one's sense that Faustus was a small-time entertainer after all.

Furthermore, Daneman's performance was too genial and open-hearted to convince one as to the scale of his revolt or the poetic justice of his punishment: Benthall seemed to treat the story as that of the misfortune of a nice chap who had experienced a thoughtless moment of rashness, and could not get himself out of the resultant mess. Presentation and performance minimised the egocentric, spiteful, irresponsible, vulgar traits in the hero: the result was to lessen the tragedy of a man in whom good and bad tendencies are inextricably mixed.

No such reservations could honestly be expressed about Clifford Williams's interpretation in 1968, or about Eric Porter's valiant attempt to suggest the medley of motives and emotions at war within the protagonist's brain. Here one had the intelligent, arrogant genius the text seems to demand, the sense of bored discontentment with the legitimate road to the glittering prizes, the enjoyment of the grotesque and the contemptuously sardonic delight in the humiliation of others. What was missing was the passionate desire for power and knowledge which lay behind the negotiations with Lucifer; like Mannering, Hardwicke and Burton before him, and Kingsley later, Porter failed to suggest the capacity of magic to 'ravish' its devotees. Nor did Williams altogether succeed in reconciling his designer's brilliantly idiosyncratic images of Hell – most notably the memorably evil Deadly Sins – with the obvious perceptive intelligence of his Faustus. The infernal machinery was perhaps a self-indulgence in the context, being too repellent to enable us to comprehend this ascetic Faustus's fascination with it. More seductive were some of the magical effects: Alexander and his Paramour were silvered statues moving in mimed dance; at the Pope's banquet a slimy grey hand appeared from His Holiness's dish; when Mephostophilis spat out a grape-seed it exploded. Like Coghill in 1957, Williams devised these ingenious routines in order to emphasise his vision of Faustus as exuberant as well as scholarly; the joy in scoring off the supreme Pontiff must be given as much weight as the pleasure of hearing Homer sing, and Williams almost made it work.

John Barton was in some respects more successful in creating a unified theme for the play, but often at some expense to its texture. The concept of the action as the diseased fantasy of a weak neurotic helped to stress the hollowness of Faustus's recompense for his sacrifice, while the use of puppets and masks cleverly reinforced the manipulation of man by devils. But, for those who reject the image of Faustus as deluded victim merely, and see him as possessing at least some of the lofty hopes and the eager spirit of enterprise of the age in which he was conceived, Barton's treatment ceased to create a sense of tragedy and declined into bathos. McKellen's Faustus was not even allowed to befool the Pope or fling the fireworks: he shrank to a twitching neurotic in a tinsel cloak, and as a result the play became a powerful study of a psychotic temperament with no counterbalancing features. The richness of the clash of conflicting values, the fascination of a personality combining disparate and warring impulses, was lost. Barton united the various elements of the original only by rejecting ambiguity.

Christopher Fettes too was able to achieve an impression of unity with his scaled-down text of 1980 and his view of the play as embodying the frustrations of a contemporary adolescent. Indeed, the work's relevance for today was perhaps exaggerated by some of the ruthless updating he permitted himself. Faustus, a 'typical' student with portable cassette recorder, smoking a cigarillo, his tutor a blind man in a wheelchair, was accompanied by a blend of classical and popular music, and a variety of sound-effects, including voices of American spacemen backing the concluding lines. Some of this seemed merely distracting. There were also worthier novelties, the most striking being the casting of David Rappaport, an actor 3 feet 6 inches tall, as the Pope. Here the notions of man's tenuous hold on temporal achievement, of the corrupt abuse of authority as a means of compensation, were more tellingly conveyed than in more conventional productions: one saw a parallel between Faustus and his adversary. Yet the play too shrank under this treatment; its full resonance was lost despite the erudite programme note's emphasis on the Greek concept of *pothos*, 'the longing for that which cannot be obtained'. *Pothos* was seen as essentially a juvenile passion: part of Faustus's triumph is surely that he never loses this longing even in his maturity.

Productions of the play have come far since *The Times* said of Poel's 1896 version, '*Dr Faustus* seems scarcely fitted for representation on the modern stage'. Few would take so gloomy a view today. Even if they have rarely been content to take the text on trust, directors can scarcely be blamed for their vigorous wielding of the scissors or the felt pen. Nor must the problems of creating a coherent Faustus, of making the notions of Hell and damnation meaningful to a modern audience, of spanning the presumed 'gulf between the peaks', be minimised. A conflation of the best features of all the productions reviewed here – Benthall's spectacle, Williams's consistent concept of a complex Faustus, Barton's puppetry, Fettes's economy (and his Mephostophilis) – might prove rewarding, but they illustrate the obvious truth that no single production of *Doctor Faustus* in recent times can be deemed truly satisfactory. Yet the play has inspired some exciting theatrical moments, and much of its power is still untapped, particularly its contemporary relevance. All who have participated in its realisation, as spectators, actors or directors, Christian or agnostic, might well unite in agreeing that this play's continuing power to move and stir us lies in Wilde's penetrating aphorism, 'When the Gods wish to punish us, they answer our prayers.'

READING LIST

Only critical works directly relating to *Doctor Faustus* are included. Place of publication is London where not stated. Asterisks denote works represented in Jump's Casebook on the play.

Nigel Alexander, 'The Performance of Marlowe's *Dr Faustus*', *Proceedings of the British Academy*, 57 (1971) pp. 331–49. Erudite stage-centred discussion of play's impact.

Max Bluestone, '*Libido Speculandi*: Doctrine and Dramaturgy in Contemporary Interpretations of Marlowe's *Doctor Faustus*', in N. Ribkin (ed.), *Reinterpretations of Elizabethan Drama* (New York and London, 1969) pp. 33–88. Impressive survey demonstrating impossibility of simplistic readings of play.

J. P. Brockbank, *Marlowe: Dr Faustus* (1962). Incisively compact introduction.*

Nicholas Brooke, 'The Moral Tragedy of Doctor Faustus', *Cambridge Journal*, 5 (1951–2) pp. 662–87. Brilliant analysis of play as 'inverted morality'.*

Cleanth Brooks, 'The Unity of Dr Faustus', in J. Lawlor and W. H. Auden (eds), *To Nevill Coghill from Friends* (1966) pp. 110–24. Defends integrity of the whole work.*

Wolfgang Clemen, *English Tragedy before Shakespeare*, trs. T. S. Dorsch (1961). Places the accent on dramatic speech.

Douglas Cole, *Suffering and Evil in the Plays of Christopher Marlowe* (Princeton, NJ, 1962). Ch. 5 relates *Faustus* to religious and dramatic traditions of its day.

T. W. Craik, 'Faustus' Damnation Reconsidered', *Renaissance Drama*, 2 (1969) pp. 188–96.

Verna Ann Foster, '*Dr Faustus* on the Stage', *Theatre Research*, 14 (1974) pp. 18–44. Invaluable survey of productions 1896–1968.

W. W. Greg, 'The Damnation of Faustus', *Modern Language Review*, 41 (1946) pp. 97–107. Staunch support for damnation as attendant on copulation with demon.*

Michael Hattaway, *Elizabethan Popular Theatre* (1982). Illuminates *Faustus* in context of stage conditions of the period.

Pauline Honderich, 'John Calvin and Dr Faustus', *Modern Language Review*, 68 (1975) pp. 1–13. Sees Faustus's inability to repent as influenced by Calvinistic determinism.

John Jump (ed.), *Marlowe: Dr Faustus*, Macmillan Casebook (1969).

Alvin Kernan (ed.), *Two Renaissance Mythmakers: Christopher Marlowe and Ben Jonson* (1977). Includes Edward A. Snow's 'Marlowe's *Dr Faustus* and the Ends of Desire'.

Nicholas Kiessling, 'Doctor Faustus and the Sin of Demoniality', *Studies in English Literature 1500–1900*, 15 (1975) pp. 205–11. Takes issue with Greg, above.

Leo Kirschbaum, 'Marlowe's *Faustus*: A Reconsideration', *Review of English Studies*, 19 (1943) pp. 225–41. Argues for orthodox Christian interpretation.*

Harry Levin, *The Overreacher* (Cambridge, Mass., 1952; London, 1954). Respected study, seeing Faustus's as 'the atheist's tragedy' but perhaps an arbitrary one.*

Charles G. Masinton, *Christopher Marlowe's Tragic Vision: A Study in Damnation* (Athens, Ohio, 1972), esp. ch. 6: 'A Devilish Exercise: Faustus and the Failure of Renaissance Man'.

J. C. Maxwell, 'The Sin of Faustus', *The Wind and the Rain*, 4 (1947) pp. 49–52.*

Robert Ornstein, 'The Comic Synthesis in *Doctor Faustus*', *English Literary History*, 22 (1955) pp. 165–72. Makes excellent case for relevance of comic scenes.*

Michael Scott, *Renaissance Drama and a Modern Audience* (1982). Ch. 2 discusses the modernity of *Doctor Faustus*.

James Smith, 'Marlowe's *Doctor Faustus*', *Scrutiny*, 8 (1939–40) pp. 36–55. Pioneering essay on the play as a morality.*

Robert Speaight, *William Poel and the Elizabethan Revival* (1954). Discusses (pp. 113–19) the productions of 1896 and 1904.

J. B. Steane, *Marlowe: A Critical Study* (Cambridge, 1964). Arbitrates sensibly between rival extremes.*

Judith Weil, *Christopher Marlowe: Merlin's Prophet* (Cambridge, 1976). Sees irony at heart of Marlowe's attitude to his protagonists.

Robert H. West, 'The Impatient Magic of Dr Faustus', *English Literary Renaissance*, 4 (1974) pp. 218–40. Reviews recent work, attempting to resolve the question of Faustus's tragic fall.

The *Tulane Drama Review*, 8:4 (Summer 1964), devoted to Marlowe, contains G. K. Hunter on Faustus's five-act structure, C. L. Barber's 'The Form of Faustus' Fortunes Good or Bad', and Jerzy Grotowski on staging the play in Poland, as well as stimulating general essays by Harry Levin, John Russell Brown and Jocelyn Powell.

INDEX OF NAMES